The Ultimate Self-Help Guide for the
Child of an Asian Tiger Mom

The Ultimate Self-Help Guide *for the* Child *of an* Asian Tiger Mom

Your Path to Finding Inner Peace

VICTORIA HA

Foreword by Tsao-Lin Moy, founder of Integrative Healing Arts

Copyright ©2024, Victoria Ha

All Rights Reserved. This book may not be reproduced in whole or in part without the written consent of the publisher, except by a reviewer who may quote brief passages in a review. Nor may any part of this book be reproduced, stored in a retrieval system, or transmitted in any form or by any means, electronic, mechanical, photocopying, recording, or other, without the written permission of the publisher.

ISBN: 979-8-218-41956-1 (Print)
ISBN: 979-8-218-41957-8 (Ebook)

Cover Design: Nate Myers
Cover Imagery: Adobe Stock

I DEDICATE THIS BOOK TO my mother, my aunties, and all the tiger-parented cubs out there. Thank you to my mother, who helped provide me with the framework to become a successful tiger cub. Thank you to Marianna, who inspired me to document my process of growth and self-worth. Thank you to Matthew and Anna, who helped to edit the book and keep me going. Thank you to Tsao for your continual words of wisdom. And a big thank you to Ray, my mentors, and my friends who continually remind me that I have more to offer than my patterns.

Contents

Foreword ix
Author's Note xiii
Chapter 1: The Picture of a Tiger Mom 1
Chapter 2: In the Eyes of a Tiger Cub 41
Chapter 3: Finding Freedom from Control 63
Chapter 4: Overcoming Criticism 103
Chapter 5: Releasing Perfectionism 121
Chapter 6: Setting Boundaries 143
Chapter 7: Lessons Learned by a Tiger Cub 171
Epilogue 179
About the Author 185

Foreword

I FIRST MET VICTORIA SEVEN years ago at an event for entrepreneurs that focused on mindset and success. Out of habit, I scanned the room, looking for other minorities and other Asians who might also be on a journey of self-discovery and personal growth. There is an unspoken "knowing" and a shared experience that comes from being Asian and American and, of course, female.

At this event, there were only three of us: Victoria, Julie (of Japanese descent), and me (Chinese mix). We connected throughout the workshop and have stayed in touch ever since. Now, whenever Victoria passes through New York City, we meet for coffee, and she tells me about her next projects—such as a TEDx talk, a speech at Oxford University, a book, a new business, building a house, and creating the life that she wants—all the things she does while navigating the complexity of being a successful Asian American female.

The Ultimate Self-Help Guide for the Child of an Asian Tiger Mom

I am a first-generation Asian American female of mixed heritage (Chinese and white). In Asian culture, there is a strict hierarchy based on gender and birth rank. For example, my oldest male cousin was free to tell his younger siblings what to do. My younger cousins would tell me stories of their eldest aunt, who demanded their mother "obey" her and keep her children in the house while visiting. I suppose there is a kind of underlying purpose to this kind of hierarchy. Everyone has a birth order, and each person knows their place in the family structure. As long as everyone adheres to the rules, there is peace.

While I didn't have a tiger mom, I did have a Chinese father who was traditional and stoic. He had managed to overcome the language barrier and get into medical school, and he started a medical practice in New York. He would express disappointment at my lack of As and would compare me and my siblings to his patients' children, who were getting scholarships to Yale and Harvard.

My aunties disapproved of the fact that my siblings and I did not speak Chinese or demonstrate the proper way to address them according to the pecking order. Their sighs and disapproving comments were directed toward my father, who was the youngest of his siblings; however, because he was successful, their disapproval didn't carry as much weight.

In Asian culture, family is sacred; it must always come first. I think this is so because the family provides the structure and unity necessary for survival. The importance of family structure and values is amplified when a family immigrates to the US, a country that has historically been racist toward

Asians. The threat of racism results in family "trauma pods" that manifest as extreme "controlling" behavior by parents, often including manipulation through shame and guilt. The message you get as an Asian American child of immigrants is this: Don't make trouble; keep quiet. The nail that sticks out gets hammered down.

The danger of racism is real for Asian women, especially in the West, where they are often oversexualized and overlooked for their intelligence and achievements. That's an important reason for fraught relationships between Asian immigrant parents and their daughters. There can be no hanging out with friends or unstructured time.

When Victoria shares these trying experiences from her childhood, it gives us a more nuanced understanding of the complex dynamics of the tiger-cub relationship, as do her painful descriptions of the cultural diaspora of aunties and cousins who view it as their mission to reinforce strict adherence to family values.

For this community, the stakes are high. The hopes, dreams, and opportunities that this new country offers must not be squandered. The pressure to succeed is a matter of family honor. These hopes and dreams fall especially heavily on first-generation children, whose parents both wish the best for them and demand that they be the best.

Reading about Victoria's childhood relationship with her tiger mom tugged at my heart. Parenting is a complicated responsibility. As a mother of a daughter, I, too, want the best for my child. This desire is universal. In Western culture, we see soccer moms, helicopter parents, and snowplow parents who go to great lengths to remove every obstacle or challenge for their children. But, at some point, the child becomes an adult and must renegotiate her relationship with her parents and come into her own. This is true not only for tiger moms and cubs, but for families of all cultures who wish for their children to grow up, fulfill a purpose of their own choosing, and be happy.

I hope that you will be inspired by this story of a tiger cub who dared to defy family pressure and Asian cultural norms, risking isolation and abandonment, to secure her personal freedom—and then mustered the courage to share her story. The opportunity to witness the fierce and courageous woman Victoria has become through her journey of deliverance is a gift to all tiger cubs.

I think it is also important to read this guide and take an honest look at your own parenting style. I say this not just for the sake of your children, but also for the sake of your inner child, who continues to need unconditional love and kindness.

—Tsao-Lin Moy

TSAO-LIN MOY has over twenty-one years of experience as an expert in alternative and Chinese medicine. She is the founder of Integrative Healing Arts (https://www.integrativehealingarts.com/), which utilizes Chinese medicine, acupuncture, herbal medicine, and energy healing to treat patients. Tsao's holistic approach integrates ancient Eastern philosophy and healing methods with Western scientific paradigms of health. This powerful combination helps each patient learn how to heal, so they can take charge of their health destiny.

Author's Note

WE ASIAN AMERICANS—FIRST-, second-, and sometimes even third-generation—feel tremendous pressure to be academically and professionally successful. We are typically characterized as intelligent, industrious, and fully in charge of our lives; we put enormous effort into living up to that perception. We are coached by our parents, aunties and uncles, grandparents, and the Asian community at large to stay focused, to be "model minorities." This dynamic is especially evident in the parenting style of the Asian "tiger mom." And being on the receiving end of that parenting, as a "tiger cub," comes with unique challenges and gifts.

While many of our peers in high school and college didn't know what to do with their lives, we Asian tiger-parented cubs had defined tracks to achieve success the Asian way. As an Asian American daughter, I was self-sufficient at an early age. After college, I wasn't just scraping by, eating peanut butter sandwiches and shopping at Walmart. Right out of the gate, I was living comfortably by my own means. This is typical of many Asian American daughters. (Asian American sons may be a tad more coddled at home compared to their female counterparts, but they're also expected to be self-sufficient from day one.)

Without this expectation, and the unwritten rules most of us abide by, well, we would be unexceptional. But, as model minorities, we are always trying to perfect our idea of perfection. If there's any break in our "perfectness," (i.e., if we don't do a task correctly, we don't act appropriately in a specific circumstance, we don't say the right thing), our upbringing means we're highly self-critical, automatically correcting our actions to make ourselves appear "better" to the outside world. It sounds good. In reality, this cycle becomes degenerative to our overall well-being.

We perpetuate the classic stereotype of the model minority that comes from a perfect family and leads a perfect life. We smile and agree with many of the things that we are told. We are expected to never disagree. We marry perfectly. Admitting weakness—any flaw or mistake—wouldn't just let down our parents, our grandparents, or our family lineage. It would let down the entire Asian American community.

And this is why so many of us Asian tiger cubs feel displaced. We feel like we have to stifle who we are and what we can do, because of the critical voice—that *inner* critic, typically the voice of our mother—that runs our lives. This critic shapes our personal journeys—and it shaped my life in

Author's Note

a way that both helped me and hindered me. In fact, my story is probably very similar to your story.

My mother was completely unlike the "traditional" American homemaker. Rather than cooking and cleaning, she had a duty to make her kids high-achieving, self-sufficient, and (seemingly) most importantly, above-average. My twin sister Sabrina and I each had goals to hit and intrinsic motivations to drive us forward, and we would stop at nothing to achieve what we had set out to do. Whether in academics or in our careers, we both set out for greatness.

In my adulthood, I fulfilled all the expectations that my Asian tiger parents had of me. I was a millionaire by the age of thirty, and I had a large house in a desirable area on the "right" side of town. And, in my forties, I was a successful businesswoman earning seven figures. I was the dream of every Asian parent and the poster child of the Asian tiger cub.

But the tiger parenting that had worked so well in my childhood and my early twenties had stopped working for me as I grew older. The facade of "good" parenting had fallen away. The drive my mother had instilled in me to seek more and achieve more had started to reveal its flaws. My personal life was tragic—a blank canvas of nothingness, simply because it hadn't been developed. I became a robot, repeating flawed patterns in my relationships and my work life because I had known those patterns intimately from birth.

From the outside, it looked like I had it all. But, in my heart, I knew that I was setting myself up for failure. My mind and body were screaming, *Stop doing this.* I wanted a life that was more fulfilled, more joyous than the one my parents were living (which it looked like they didn't enjoy). Yet the rote actions I continued to perform were from my childhood; they had been learned from my parents' interactions with each other and with me, and I didn't know anything else.

I needed to find a balance between how I had grown up and what I truly desired—while simultaneously navigating my tiger mom and the rest of my family. I wanted to act on how I wished my life would be, rather than continuously filling the role my parents had created for me.

Throughout my childhood, my dad had said to me, "Victoria, do what you want to do. We just want you to be happy." Yet the subtext was that, even if I was happy doing something, if my parents disapproved of it, their answer would ultimately be *no*. So I didn't know what my "new life" could be. That path had never been clear to me before.

I am sure I spent what amounts to hundreds of thousands of dollars—and years on end—on various types of therapies in my attempt to get that critical "tiger mom" voice out of my head—to find my *own* voice, my *own* path. But it was hard because, if I was happy doing something that I wanted to do, my parents never approved. It showed in their actions and their disapproving stares. (Plus, there were the comments from my aunties.) And when my parents didn't approve of what I was doing, my own desires—my own voice—took a back seat, and I dropped back into the role that I had been given at birth: living in their expectations of what and who I should be in my community's eyes. My inner critic, specifically my mother's voice, kept me continually living in this same role,

Author's Note

with the same patterns and the same traits that I had carried with me most of my life.

Eventually, I realized that this cycle didn't have to continue. I learned that I could break the cycle by silencing that inner critic. Through the silence, I ultimately found freedom. The freedom to feel my heart's true wishes, to laugh freely, and to love fully. I worked hard for this freedom, and I released the shame and guilt of betraying my parents' expectations. And it hasn't been easy. Sure, there are still actions that I take that cause me to fear judgment from others. And there are still days when I slip up and make choices strictly to please others (not just my parents, but my aunties and the community). However, those days happen more rarely now. And the good news is that you can break the cycle, too. You can find your voice—find your freedom—while also balancing the need to respect your culture and your family.

This book is my personal narrative of how to break the cycle, silence your inner critic, and find freedom. In this book, I've compiled my experiences—which I've worked for years to find solutions for—into a self-help guide for the children of Asian tiger moms. It is designed to be comprehensive, but it is probably not complete, because I am still learning and growing. I've found, though, after talking with other Asian tiger cubs, that it incorporates most of the traits, patterns, and triggers to be aware of. And I've coupled those with practical exercises that I've found helpful in avoiding slipping into the patterns and roles that my parents had assigned to me.

While you go through this process of finding your voice, keep in mind that exploring your new self and trying these exercises may create some nasty reactions. You may get the stink eye or the stare at first. You may get a tongue-lashing or the "you are embarrassing me" speech. But I promise you that it's worth the effort to try. It was for me.

Yours truly,
Vic

CHAPTER 1

The Picture of a Tiger Mom

AS ASIAN TIGER CUBS, we have been fundamentally shaped by our tiger moms. If you saw me walking down the street, you'd see an ordinary Asian American woman who grew up in a big city. Petite, five feet two inches, 105 pounds. Oftentimes, my hair is in a ponytail, and I'm usually wearing Lululemon leggings and sweatshirt as I'm just coming back from a run or a workout. For the most part, I'm perfectly poised, passionate when it comes to my ideals, and well-traveled. I drive my Porsche Macan and live in a well-to-do neighborhood. From the outside, my life could be considered the ideal American dream. But what you can't see is the confusion and the mess that's within. When I smile, the light you'd see in other people's eyes somehow isn't there. When I laugh politely, it's because I don't want to tell you that what you said was inappropriate or offensive. Authenticity doesn't come easily, because I'm wracked with thoughts of self-deprecation and worrying about ways I could do and/or be better. And all of this is because of my upbringing—that of being parented by a tiger mom.

To understand our experiences as tiger cubs, we must first take a deeper look at our tiger moms. An article by the American Psychological Association notes that Amy Chua, author of the memoir *Battle Hymn of the Tiger Mother*, defines tiger moms as "mothers of Chinese (or other ethnic) origin who are highly controlling and authoritarian, denying their children free time, play dates and extracurricular activities in order to drive them to high levels of success at any cost, unlike the softer and more forgiving Western parenting style. This stereotypical and caricature-like image seems to confirm the worst fears about Asian parenting—that it is excessively controlling, harsh and demanding unquestioning obedience with little to no concern for the child's needs, wishes or emotional well-being."[1]

My particular flavor of tiger mom was that of a Filipinos woman who had immigrated to the US from the Philippines when she was about ten. She was one of six sisters, second to the youngest, and she had lived most of her childhood in the Philippines. I remember her telling me stories about my grandfather (nicknamed Chicago) and his restaurant

---

1. Linda P. Juang, Desiree Baolin Qin, and Irene J. K. Park, "Beyond the Battle Hymn to Empirical Research on Tiger Parenting," *Society for Research on Adolescence*, https://www.s-r-a.org/index.php?option=com_dailyplanetblog&view=entry&category=teachingadolescence&id=77:beyond-the-battle-hymn-to-empirical-research-on-tiger-parenting#:~:text=According%20to%20Amy%20Chua%2C%20tiger,at%20any%20cost%2C%20unlike%20the.

business. Chicago was among the first group of minorities to go to America, specifically Chicago, to learn about cooking and the restaurant business. It was a privilege back then to travel because most Filipinos were too poor to travel abroad, and especially because of the rising tensions in the Pacific leading up to World War II. My grandfather then returned to Manila to open multiple restaurants, with the president of the Philippines and his staff frequenting his restaurants and calling them their favorites.

He served the Filipino government until the start of World War II. As favorites of the president and the executives in power, my grandparents had been fortunate enough to receive new technologies, such as the first icebox on the island, and they were one of the first families on the island to have a car and electricity. But when the Japanese invaded the Philippines, my grandfather and his family became high on the wanted list by the Japanese government. When the war hit, my grandfather's restaurants became overrun by the Japanese, and his family was forced into hiding at their country home in the outskirts in Laoag, where they stayed for many years.

During that time, my grandfather escaped to the United States. He was resourceful, and he realized that the US was taking in immigrants to work as laborers on Hawaiian plantations. He was denied entry multiple times because he had never done physical labor, yet after three attempts—and after pumicing his hands to appear more rugged—he was finally allowed to board a ship and become an electrician on a plantation on Kauai, where after seven years, he was able to bring his family as well.

While I would say that my mom's life in hiding was a rough one, according to my mother and my aunts—depending on whom you talk with—the reality was actually magical (even in a time when poverty overran the country). Although my grandmother was forced to raise her five daughters alone, each daughter had a maid, and my grandmother had house servants. There were times when my aunts and my mother had to go into hiding because the Japanese were searching the property in response to a warrant against my grandfather. But most days were filled with songs, music from the piano, lessons from tutors, and camaraderie between the sisters. And, even though my grandmother had servants to help her with the cooking, cleaning, and other household chores, she wanted to ensure that her daughters were raised properly with a good education, good morals, and strong motivation. She protected her daughters when my grandfather was away, helping them hide when the farm was searched and protecting them from thieves or any other harm that might come their way. My grandmother had a will made of iron, and for my mother and her aunts, it had imprinted on them what parenting was supposed to be: a firm hand, a stern demeanor, and a "loving" attitude to ensure that her daughters were well cared for. (Does this sound familiar to you?) As a single parent, my grandmother was a strong female role model during the formative years of my mom's life. It was common for the words "I love you" to be uttered right before a complaint or correction was issued.

All of that changed when my grandfather summoned his family to Kauai. One day, seven years to the day after my grandfather had left, my grandmother received plane tickets and a letter telling her that it was time to come to what my grandfather called "paradise." He had "made it." He had worked his way up to become the supervisor on a plantation and was one of the top men running their operations. Little did my grandmother and my aunts know that running the plantation meant actually running the main house of the plantation, and that when they came to the US, they also would have to run the main house as maidservants, a grand contrast to their previous lifestyle.

And so my mother (along with her sisters and my grandmother) stepped on a plane at the age of ten to come to the US. She never would have expected that she would go from a well-to-do life in the Philippines to that of an immigrant working as a housemaid responsible for dusting, setting the table, and ensuring that the plantation house was in order. So that was my mother's youth until she received a scholarship to college. During that time, she (along with my aunts) was poor by today's American standards—too poor to buy clothes on a regular basis, too poor to have a car, and too poor to go to college—but she was rich enough to have food on the table every day.

Given my mom's upbringing, it was somewhat understandable that she would have a sense of harshness about her and would want to raise us to be accomplished, and to give us the same and more of what she had been given, out of love and respect for us. Her parenting style, however, just didn't fit the '70s and '80s era of free love when I was growing up. While my mother wanted to give us the best of everything that she didn't have when she was growing up, we ultimately learned how to struggle, strive, and work hard.

We also learned about the importance of guilt, shame, and pride. She created an idea in our minds that we didn't deserve what we were given, whether material or emotional. We had to earn everything, instead of just receiving it like all of the other kids did. The emotional component of warm fuzzies and the traditional American definition of "love" wasn't there. Instead, the harshness of her words and her perpetual need for us to do better took its place. And that formed my mother's style of tiger parenting. It was as if something had been ingrained within her, as with other Asian mothers, that forced her to make rules and command absolutes. If you look at your mom's upbringing, would you find similar patterns?

Unlike American culture that sets out clear rules and guidelines, we are always left guessing what our tiger moms' commands mean. From birth, my sister Sabrina and I were continually guessing on how we were supposed to act, how we were supposed to gain approval from our parents, and how we could be accepted and feel loved by our community. This is due in part to Asians having a typically high-context culture in which gesture, body language, eye contact, pitch, intonation, word stress, the use of silence, and a person's status and age are as important as the actual words being spoken in conversation. On the other hand, what we know as American culture is steeped in a low-context communication style where rules are spelled out and Americans communicate primarily through spoken language. So, for us tiger cubs, actions and words become much more impactful because we have to guess the rules and function within boundaries that aren't spelled out for us.

Looking more deeply, I've noticed that this communication style is ingrained in Asian traditions and cultures. When we think of "Asian culture," American society tends to think of Chinese or Southeast Asian people. The reality is that Asia is made up of over forty-eight countries from Burma, Pakistan, Turkey, India, Iran, and Thailand to China, the United Arab Emirates, and the Philippines. And, while each culture of Asia is uniquely different with their own character traits, holidays, mannerisms, and forms of hospitality, there tends to be a shared way of parenting when they come to the United States. Maybe it's an immigrant story, but after talking to so many people, I've found that it's a uniquely Asian way of parenting.

If you saw my mother today, you'd think of her as one of those sweet women you see on the streets in Chinatown. She looks like one of those dolls whose head is made out of a dried Granny Smith apple. She appears to be kind, her eyes brimming with a smile; however, inside, she's what my friend Paull calls a "wily snake with a harsh tongue." Because of her upbringing, and the stark change from her life in the Philippines to her life in Kauai, she has had to constantly battle to earn her keep, and she's been this harsh most of her adult life, although her harshness has dissipated with age.

At just over five feet tall, my mother is a short woman who makes up for her small stature with her big attitude. While funny in her own right, she can also be extremely paranoid and judgmental. She oftentimes will look down on other people, making vocal judgments about everyone around her—typically with an air of unintentional superiority—as if she knows best. For example, she can easily assume the worst of people based on their clothing and their actions. On many occasions, my mother has glanced at another Asian woman at a Chinese grocery store while picking fruit, and she has made a judgment in an instant: "Yuck! That's a terrible piece of fruit!" She'd scrunch her nose and drop the unwanted piece of fruit back into the bin with a heavy thud. She can also dress someone down with just a look and a comment such as, "Her clothes are too tight; she shouldn't wear that. She looks like a prostitute," or, "Look at her shoes. She must have gotten them from Payless. They are cheap." Like many Asian tiger moms, my mom thinks that she is fundamentally right in all circumstances—and she openly voices her opinion, even when it's disrespectful or out of place. And, as a well-respected teacher, she has amplified this trait and asserted it upon her students as well.

She likes to always keep busy, and she often does tasks by herself because others can't do them to meet her expectations. For example, she will make dinner, have dinner with us, and then clean up afterward because *nobody* can do it better than she can. Sometimes, she adds a bit of martyrdom when that happens, crying about it because we're not helping her—but when we do help her, we never live up to her expectations.

The Picture of a Tiger Mom

She constantly nitpicks my father, to whom she has been married for more than fifty years, oftentimes criticizing him in a nagging, annoying voice about everything from the way he eats ("Pat, you are eating too fast," or, "Pat, slow down. Chew your food," or, "Pat, you shouldn't be eating that,") to how he dresses ("Pat, don't wear that. Go change; your shirt is holey,") and how he puts away the dishes ("That's not clean. I hate how I have to do everything myself.")

Within all of this criticism there is an expectation for perfection. I was definitely not perfect, but I tried to be—especially in my mother's eyes. The behaviors that were exhibited in my mother's actions more or less manifested themselves in a set of unwritten rules. And while I earnestly tried to understand and abide by these rules when I was younger, they long remained a mystery to me. Now, after years of gaining perspective and wisdom, I have finally gained some clarity on these rules, which I have compiled into this list:

1. Firstly, ensure your cubs are polite and stay silent, no matter what. Don't speak up.

As a child, I'd often be a tad too vocal about my opinions, and I'd hear my mom crying about my vociferous nature. It was Sabrina's and my duty to be "nice" to other people, mind our manners, and not say anything, because it was "unladylike" and wholly un-Asian to behave otherwise. A common saying that my mom would utter was that "rude Caucasians won't be successful growing up because of their manners." My desire to succeed by adhering to the "Asian way" was intense, as I (like all tiger cubs) wanted to make my tiger mom proud.

The Ultimate Self-Help Guide for the Child of an Asian Tiger Mom

I learned early to hold my tongue, after I once commented on my mother's friend's weight. It was one of my earliest memories; I was approximately six at the time. For years, my mom had a really good friend who just happened to have a weight problem. Oftentimes, my mom would comment on it at home. "I saw Jody today, and boy, she's really gained weight." Or, "Jody and I went out to lunch today to Sankura" (a local Japanese restaurant in San Bruno). "We ordered ten dishes between the two of us. I stopped eating after four dishes, but she didn't. She finished the entire meal."

Because of my mom's frequent comments, I naturally assumed that I could say something as well. I, of course, was wrong.

On that fateful day, my mother was driving her white '85 Crown Victoria station wagon to pick up Jody to take her to one of Sabrina's piano recitals. Sabrina and I sat in the back seat. Jody got into the passenger side of the car. At approximately five feet six inches tall and very stocky, she was fat by American standards and Asian standards. And when I say stocky, I mean she was very, very rotund. It was hard for her to sit comfortably in the station wagon. She wore light-blue pants with an elastic waistband that was too tight, a button-down white shirt with the buttons ready to burst, and a snug gray jacket that had been left unbuttoned. I wondered, if she buttoned her jacket, whether the buttons would hit me.

"Hi, kids," she said. She looked back at us, her short, mousy brown hair framing her rosy, cherubic face. She was quite pleasant-looking. "Are you excited to perform?"

"Yes, Jody," Sabrina and I chimed in.

"Mrs. Merod," my mom corrected us.

"Mrs. Merod," we parroted. "Thank you for coming to our recital," we recited. Our mom had taught us early in life to thank people for attending our recitals, birthdays, and other events.

After that comment, Sabrina looked out of the back-seat window. I, however, didn't. From my vantage point, I could see what Mom had been talking about. Jody was a really, really big person. Before my mother started the car, I unbuckled my seat belt, leaned forward, and whispered loudly to my mom, "Mom, you're right. She is large."

I was proud of myself for being observant, for saying something accurate, and I thought that I'd get a round of kudos for agreeing with my mom on her judgment. However, the moment after the words left my mouth, I could feel my mother shrink in her seat. No doubt, even though I had whispered, Jody had heard me.

"Victoria, sit down and wear your seat belt." Mom gave me a withering look—one of those looks that could kill. She noticed Jody's wide-eyed, hurt expression and said, "Don't mind her. Kids." She laughed uncomfortably, then made some small talk as we drove south to San Mateo. Sabrina was wise to just look out the window and keep her mouth shut.

After that comment, it was hard for me to concentrate on my performance or feel excited about performing. I knew that I would probably be punished later that day, as was often the case when I said something that was not pleasing to my mother's ears. I fretted about what I had said on the car ride over, and it impacted me during my performance. While I had spent countless hours rehearsing on my piano, I froze when it came to my turn on stage, and I played wrong notes during half of the piece. Sure enough, in addition to the tongue-lashing my mother gave me for my poor performance, she washed out my mouth with an Ivory soap bar and water because I had said something offensive to her friend. It took me a few more times, a few more lessons, to learn to hold my tongue. But I eventually learned.

2. Ensure your cubs have strict guidance and receive commensurate punishments for things that embarrass you, as their mother. This will make them into better people.

Tiger moms are terrific at setting boundaries and being strict. Handing out punishments and laying on guilt are the tried-and-true methods for getting the cubs in line. Often, as I was growing up, I would ask the question, "Why?" The typical answer I got was: "Because I said so." This seemed to do the trick between the ages of zero and four; but as my sister and I got older, that answer was no longer sufficient. If we asked inappropriate questions or were too inquisitive, we would get punished—and I was punished a lot.

One day, my sister accidentally found our dad's condoms. What is a tiger mom to do in that scenario? There really is no parenting guide. Sabrina and I must have been only five or six years old at the time. We were in our parents' bedroom, as that was where the second TV was. Mom had wanted to use the primary television set in the living room so that she could have alone time with her favorite PBS series, and we were relegated to the bedroom.

The Picture of a Tiger Mom

Sabrina and I were sitting in our parents' room, watching some program I can't recall. At one point, Sabrina got bored, and she started exploring, as she often liked to do, and was opening their dresser drawers.

"Look what I found," said Sabrina. She held up small, plastic-wrapped squares in red, yellow, and blue. "Ribbed, for her pleasure," she read from one of the labels, not understanding what she was reading, as we had only recently begun to read.

I was intrigued. "Give me that!" I shouted, and snatched at the red square she was holding.

"Hey, it's mine! I found it. Get your own." She pointed to the drawer.

I started going through the packages, excited that there were so many colors, and that they each had a different descriptor. One read, "Designed for her pleasure." I had always wondered what made my mom happy. I knew she was usually happy when Sabrina and I behaved. But how could something inside that small package make her happy?

It was at that point when our mom walked in. Sabrina stopped in her tracks. I smiled and said, "Hey, Mom, look what Sabrina found!"

My mom was mortified. It would be a nightmare situation for any parent, let alone a tiger mom who cares about her image, her family's image, appearances, adhering to structure, and, well, abhorring anything that deviates from those ideals.

"Sabrina!" she yelled. She had the look of death in her eyes. I knew instantly that Sabrina would get punished.

Mom was angry. Sabrina became wide-eyed and started crying, knowing that she had overstepped her bounds and was in territory that she shouldn't be in.

"Come here *now*, both of you," our mother roared from the threshold. I shut the dresser drawer and reluctantly inched my way to the door with my sister following, the TV still blaring in the background.

My mom grabbed Sabrina's arm and dragged her down the hall. "You are a bad girl. *Bad* girl."

"Mom. What were those? They looked like candy. Was it candy?"

My mom felt super embarrassed. How was she to explain what the condoms were for?

At that point, my mother sat horrified and couldn't explain anything. "Let's go." She dragged Sabrina into our room. Sabrina then proceeded to get fifteen very loud and very hard spanks.

Watching from the doorway in fascination, I was relieved that I hadn't been the instigator, and I also felt a tad bit guilty that I had partaken in the fun. At that very early age, I was learning to not ask questions and to keep my mouth shut at all times.

Sabrina was so traumatized that she stayed home from school the next day. It permanently distorted Sabrina's view of sex. While we didn't talk about that moment until we were almost eighteen, the scars of it had stunned us to not do much or say much, but whenever Sabrina and I bring up that moment, we always laugh and make light of our mother's overreaction to embarrassment. As adults looking through a Western lens, it is easier for us to see the duality of the traumatic event: our mom's sheer embarrassment from her daughters finding condoms, and the shame that came with it because of her Eastern upbringing. When faced with shame or embarrassment, it was easier for our mom to hide or lash out to show that she was in control. It also gave us unspoken but clear direction on how we should think about sex and what the consequences would be.

3. *Control your cubs with extracurricular activities.*

Oftentimes, you'll see tiger moms transporting their cubs to dance lessons, violin lessons, and Chinese lessons. While Americans can't fathom this Asian way of relaxing and playing, for me and my sister, having a steady schedule like this brought a lot of comfort; and, in turn, it allowed us to build the skills and discipline we have to this day. For my mother, it gave her the comfort of knowing where we were at all times, in addition to knowing that we were learning life skills and would be more advanced with our developmental and learning skills. For example, did you know that playing music helps the young develop brain function?

Like that of many Asian-parented children, our household was very strict with activities. We were always kept busy, and our weekdays and weekends were highly structured compared to those of our peers. Monday through Friday, we'd go to school and participate in student government. After school was when the real rigor began:

- From 2:30–5:00 p.m.: After-school sports (for me, this was cross-country and track; for Sabrina, it was cheerleading)
- Tuesdays or Thursdays at 5:30 p.m.: Music lessons (Sabrina played the oboe and piano, while I played the viola, flute, and guitar)
- Every day: Practice at least one instrument a day for at least an hour
- Every day: Study and do homework for one to three hours until done

Weekends consisted of:
- California Youth Symphony (CYS) rehearsal
- Quartet rehearsal
- Playing at recitals and gigs at weddings and other types of festive receptions
- Dinner with either immediate family or extended family every Sunday

Sometimes, we'd fit hanging out with friends in there, but this schedule didn't leave much time for dating or just enjoying life. However, within all that structure there was a kind of freedom. For the most part, once we knew what our structure was for the day or for the week, we could plan within those restrictions. For example, on every other Saturday, I had a three-hour quartet practice with my longtime friends Gerry (violinist), Cory (violinist), and Victoria (cellist). As long as we rehearsed part of the time, we could do whatever we wanted in the hours that remained when we weren't rehearsing. The allotted time didn't dictate how exactly we spent our time—what mattered was that we spent our time doing something, and hopefully something productive.

On Saturday mornings, Sabrina and I also had free time to watch cartoons from 8:00 to 10:00 before we did our chores. And once our chores were done, Saturday was our one day to be lazy before we began our Sunday-through-Friday structure. We would go on long walks at noon, go on picnics, and go to the farmers market. It was also on those days that we would dream of having different lives where we wouldn't have to go to California Youth Symphony all the time, where we didn't have to feel discontent with where we were in life. We viewed our time growing up as a prison of sorts; it was so structured that we felt like we couldn't breathe. But, within that structure, there were instances of fun. For example, our foursome for quartet practice was fun. And when we went to a gig to play, we'd giggle and pretend we were the ones dancing and having a good time. The music would enter our souls, filling us from the inside, helping us to feel every part of us so that we could bring it to life.

This structure has continued to be an important part of my life as an adult. When I have a lot of unstructured free time, my mind tends to wander. As a result, I don't get as much accomplished, and I end up feeling like a petrified rock. While there are days when I need that, the reality is that when I don't have structure, I tend to be pulled in a million pieces. As Mom always said, "Idle mind, idle thoughts. And that gets you nowhere in life." This motto has stuck with me; and, in a way, it motivates me to this day. People have asked me how I have been able to achieve as much as I have, and the reality is that it's because I had the structure in place that I learned in my childhood to create the dreams and life that I now have. Just like I did in grade school and youth symphony, I can show up as I need to be, I plan my days accordingly and within the confines of my schedule, and then I have the choice to do something fun, or show up angry or sad or anything in between. And when I don't have that structure, my day is spent sometimes surfing the internet for news, reading Facebook, and doing other unhelpful things that keep me from feeling productive.

4. *Criticism builds character.*

Our tiger moms are overly critical for the sake of "providing input." While our friends got the big bear hugs and the kisses after the boo-boos, we got the critical eye and the critical voice that was necessary to teach us cubs to see things "differently."

My mom often called my friends' parents' parenting styles "soft." She'd say, "Your friends are all soft. Their parents aren't preparing them for the real world. Don't think of what I'm telling you as criticism. Think of it as helpful feedback to help you improve. And, if I didn't provide input now, just think of what you'd create, who you'd be."

I don't ever remember hearing her say "Good job," or, "I'm so proud of you," when I was growing up. Instead, I heard, "You can do better," or, "No! Don't do this, do that." Sometimes, my mother would give me helpful suggestions such as, "This would have been better if you'd done this instead."

To non-Asians, a dirty look might be interpreted as a dig or a threat, as though the person was saying, "Oh, look at that, she could have done X, Y, or Z." But from a tiger mom, that dirty look of disdain is given to her cub as a way of criticizing them for their own good. This was my mother's way of helping us to do something differently when she found us behaving in a misguided way. It was her way of saying, "Oh, let me help you do X, Y, or Z."

Once, when I was eight, I asked my dad why my mom always criticized me. At the time, we were staying with my Aunt Eddie at her house in San Jose. My aunt was watching us while my mom was in Washington, DC, to receive the Christa McAuliffe Prize for her work as a teacher. I had just gotten off the phone with my mother who, from two thousand miles away, was wondering why I hadn't yet finished my schoolwork. I still had two more assignments that needed to be done that night.

When I posed my question to my dad, he replied, "Victoria, she's not criticizing you. She's just trying to help you. Guide you."

"But I want to receive compliments too. I want to get hugged, to feel loved. Don't I deserve that?" I asked.

"It's not that Mom doesn't love you. She does. But she's not the one who is supposed to give you hugs all the time. She's not that type of person. But I'm always here for the hugs, Vic. We love you."

Not satisfied with my dad's response, Aunt Eddie looked at me sternly and replied, "Vic, it's not about deserving something or not deserving something. Do you think we deserved to become maids? No. Do you think we deserved this life? No. But compliments, Vic? Please. Compliments don't get you anywhere. If you want a hug, that's what your dad is for. All of us are here to guide you because you need the help. We wouldn't be here if you didn't need the help."

Dad added, "Mom means well. You just need to come to me. I love you, Vic. I'm always here for you." He gave me a hug that was intended to cheer me up, but ultimately it just depressed me. To me, my dad's words meant that my mother would never be the type of mother my friends had—a vocal and positive cheerleader who encouraged their young at every part of the journey. That was my dad's role.

After that conversation, I didn't feel like going to my dad for support or going home with him to Millbrae. While I loved that Western emotional quality in my father, I wanted to hear those words of encouragement from my mother who could never give that emotional nurturing to me. Instead, it was all about performance and doing and being better, being more accomplished than others.

Oftentimes, my mother—like all proud Asian tiger mothers who show off their young—made us perform at church. She thought it was prudent to give an offering to God of her children's gifts, as they were "celebrations of God." And she believed that God wouldn't have given us our innate abilities if he didn't want us to perform for the "glory of God." Being trained at such an early age, we often enjoyed performing, primarily because we could listen to the notes and tune out the glares and stares of the crowd. We'd criticize ourselves in private, hearing our mother's words echo in our minds as we homed in on a wrong note or an incorrect vibrato. But what we hated most was hearing our mother's feedback. We preferred to hear our own critical "mother" voice in our heads.

For example, one day at church, Sabrina and I played an étude by Bach, a duet on the flute and oboe. It wasn't our best performance, as we did not have the same syncopation in some sections and we missed a few notes. The congregation, however, gave us a standing ovation while our mother glared. On this occasion (as on many others), she told us that we could have done better—but this particular escapade was a bit more harsh than usual. We could tell that she was genuinely embarrassed by our performance. Afterward, she just said, "You didn't smile. This wasn't your best performance. I know you thought that was a good job, but I heard at least ten wrong notes. I'm not sure your grandfather would be proud." If it were just our own inner critics we had to face, we could cringe and move on. But those words had come directly from our mother; and over time, the reverberation of her disapproval wore on until we could not only hear her words but see her critical glare and feel her judgment and disapproval. It would eventually seep into our minds, making us feel and act like we didn't belong to our classes or the organizations we joined, like we were unworthy of receiving As or getting the jobs we eventually had or created.

My mother would bring up my grandfather's name on rare occasions when she wanted to make a particularly impactful statement, because his name would elicit fear, and because my grandfather had unattainable expectations for both of us. When growing up, we'd go back to Kauai every summer to spend time with my grandparents. It was during those times when Grandpa Pascual would want us to play the piano, the violin, or the flute as he loved to hear music; and, more importantly, he loved to hear us play music. Depending on how well we played, we'd get anywhere from a quarter to a dollar. Sometimes, he'd give us five dollars. He'd let us know, however, that if we played really well, we'd get twenty dollars. Regardless of how we played, he'd always say, "You are good girls" in his Filipino accent. We always wanted to please him, to do better. So, when Mom mentioned our grandfather in her criticism, her comment made us realize that we could have—and should have—done better, that we should have practiced more or done something more than what we did to prepare for that fateful Sunday.

In situations like this, it was obvious that her comments were never meant to hurt us, but to help us succeed. This was because, according to the Chinese culture, we needed to succeed and become self-sufficient in the world. If our parents didn't want us to succeed, they wouldn't have found the time to criticize us in the first place. As a child, I learned to brush myself off and be that much better than the rest. My mom's harsh criticisms were given out of love; they were meant to help us succeed. Regardless of society's messaging that told us we needed praise, criticism was her form of praise—albeit not the American way. So, while by American standards our household could have been considered void of emotional or psychological stability, we knew that our childhood was designed for our success; it was different from the emotional stability that other people had, but we were being desensitized for the real world.

Therefore, even without the emotional nurturing that I so wanted, growing up, I knew that my mother loved me. She was preparing me to succeed—financially, if not functionally—in society. On the other hand, I wasn't prepared for emotional or psychological stability later in life, even though my father had said that he would provide the encouragement in the form that I wanted. I had to find that on my own. I became desensitized to the need for praise. If I craved a kind word, it was because I was "soft." I was told that I wouldn't be prepared for the real world because the real world didn't work that way. So I would often sit there and listen to my mother's harsh words, thinking that they were making me better. Better than average. Better than everyone else.

5. *The people you keep around you are reflections of you.*
In a tiger mom's eyes, there is always a level of comparison and competition between her cubs and those around them. For me, this was amplified because I'm a twin. Just imagine growing up with someone who looks like you, has the same mannerisms as you, and is better than you because she gets higher grades and is slated for valedictorian. That was my twin, Sabrina. And while some might think that having a twin could be fun, for us, it was also built-in competition. Not only did I have to worry about what my mother thought, but I became that much more obsessed with doing better and being better, because I wanted to be the "good" twin, the "better" twin. Sabrina and I had a friendly competition when we were younger, and it wasn't until we were in our early forties that we started to develop a healthy, loving relationship. It's no surprise

that when Sabrina passed her GMAT, I passed my LSAT. When Sabrina went to get her MBA, I went to law school. When Sabrina got married, our parents wanted me to get married… and I ultimately got married two years later. The exact year that Sabrina had Mattie, her first child, I got divorced. And, while I'd like to say that it was the competitive environment of the Bay Area, or that it was a natural "twin" thing, the reality was that our competitive dynamic was fostered at home.

Growing up, whenever one of us got an A+, our mother would praise us. However, if one of us got an A-, our mother would shame us. It was like one of those bad Asian movies where a mother shows her excitement by pointing out her child's strengths and weaknesses to the world. When we were in middle school and high school, Sabrina and I had a self-imposed, strict schedule for when our mother would look at our work, critique it, and improve it before we could hand it in. In one particular case, Sabrina and I had been given an assignment to write and create collages on our favorite states (hers being California, and mine being Hawaii). Always the eager beaver, Sabrina finished her project quickly, completing the collage of the state bird, tree, and flag, and writing a five-page report in less than one day. She was so proud of her efficiency and the quality of her work. Mine, on the other hand, was a crude outline that I had scrambled to complete to reach our self-imposed deadline. Because Sabrina was so excited about her project, she let our mother know of her completion. And when Mom asked for mine, I got only a glare. She ended up completing the project for me, disapproving of my every move along the way.

This scrutiny and competition applied to my friends as well. Instead of viewing a friend as simply a friend, I sized them up, doing a once-over to assess my "opponent," a skill I'd learned from my Asian aunties. In a single glance I would assess a few things: *Is she dressed appropriately? Does she groom herself? What brand of shoes does she wear, and how much did they cost? What brand of handbag does she carry? What is her demeanor? How does she talk? Does she speak in broken English, or does she have polished English, the type of speech that comes from a boarding school?* In that moment I could assess if the person was lower-, middle-, or upper-class, and how I stacked up against them from a socioeconomic perspective. I'd ask myself: *Will I benefit from knowing this person? Does this person fit within my network of friends? Is she friendworthy? Will my family consider this person acceptable?*

Once, when I was seven, I brought home my friend Anne from school. With bright red hair and a freckled face, she had a lively demeanor that was different from the other girls at Crystal Springs Elementary School. We braided each other's hair and played tag on the playground. The problem was that my mom thought that Anne was unacceptable. Mom picked us up from school, intending to take us to get ice cream before we headed home to play. As I opened the car door and excitedly scooted over to give Anne room, I saw my mom give her a once-over. In that moment, the smile on my mom's face turned to a look of stone. I knew that she had deemed Anne to be unacceptable. Wearing her brother's grungy hand-me-downs, my friend looked scrappy. To my mother, being friends with someone who couldn't wear decent clothes was like being friends with the Clampetts from *The Beverly Hillbillies*. It wasn't that my mother thought we were superior; she believed that we would be judged by the people we surrounded ourselves with, and she needed to ensure that they reflected well onto us.

6. *Ensure your cubs apologize, even if they don't know what they are apologizing for.*

As Asians, if we don't apologize, then… well, we're not Asian. Culturally, Asians have a way of deferring to the collective voice. If we don't agree with the collective, we're automatically wrong; and, oftentimes, we're punished and are expected to apologize for our "wrongdoing." This is a uniquely Asian dynamic. As a kid, I was "wrong" a lot because I had a very strong and unique voice. In fact, I feel like I began apologizing from the moment I was born.

There were so many instances of this, but the one that sticks out most happened when I was five or six years old. Sabrina and I had a big, bouncy blue ball that we could get into and roll around the house. We loved that thing. It was our "car" as we rolled from room to room. We grew up in a split-level house that was divided by a single stairway that led to the first floor. While we were allowed to aimlessly wander around in our bouncy ball, our mom hadn't said anything specifically about going down the stairs. So I was curious as to what the experience would be like.

"Sabrina, what you would say if we went down the stairs?" (Interpretation: "Sabrina, I'm pushing you down the stairs. Let me know what it's like. If you don't get hurt, and you enjoy it, I'll do it, too!" I was always making my sister experience things first.)

"OK! We can do this."

So Sabrina gingerly got into the blue ball, and I pushed her down the stairs in it. Yes, of course, there were some screams, but I heard shrieks of delight as well.

The ball thudded down the red shag-carpeted stairs, stopping at the door at the bottom of the stairway.

"And? Should I do it?" I yelled down.

Sabrina stuck her hand out of the blue ball and gave me a thumbs-up. So I started going down the stairs to help her bring the ball up so that I could roll down, too.

It was at this point when our tiger mom came looking for us as we were supposed to be studying. Our mother had been attempting to have us learn another language—Chinese—at the age of five or six, but it was turning out to be a failed experiment as neither of us wanted to do it. Not only were we poor students (which made her look bad), but it was hard to juggle another set of lessons alongside dance, piano, and violin lessons; GATE (gifted and talented education) classes; and day care.

"Victoria! Sabrina!" our mother screamed. Apparently, she had heard the loud thud of Sabrina hitting the door.

I remember looking up mid-stair as I was crawling down toward Sabrina, who was standing next to the ball by the door. She didn't say anything.

As our mom looked at us, she was horrified by what she saw: her two daughters both looked guilty about doing something that they shouldn't be doing, while avoiding the

Chinese lessons that they hated and that she had commanded them to do.

"Get up here. What happened?"

Both Sabrina and I scrambled up the stairs.

"She pushed me!" said Sabrina tearfully.

"Are you hurt?" Mom asked.

"I got a couple of bruises." She pointed to her elbow and her knee as I rolled my eyes. (It was obvious that Sabrina was making it all up. She had literally been screaming with delight moments before, when she'd rolled down the stairs.)

Mom patted Sabrina's bruises while Sabrina feigned distress. I seemed to always get the short end of the stick.

"Victoria, apologize to Sabrina!" Mom said sternly.

"I'm sorry, Sabrina," I said, not meaning it.

"For what, Victoria?"

"I'm sorry for pushing you down the stairs," I said. Under my breath, I muttered, "Even though you enjoyed it."

Mom heard that. She looked at me. "You are getting a spanking." And I got thirty spankings that day.

While, in this instance, I didn't fully understand the rule I was being forced to apologize for breaking, there were of course other times when I apologized because I knew that I had intentionally caused someone harm. For example, our cousin Paul and I once conspired to put Tabasco sauce on our older cousin Kate's thumb. Kate was still an avid thumb-sucker at the age of twelve (we were ten at the time). We decided that, when Kate took a nap, we would put Tabasco sauce on her thumb. After Paul had slipped five drops onto her thumb, we ran to the other room.

The Picture of a Tiger Mom

Of course, Kate woke up hysterically crying because her thumb and her mouth were on fire. And, even though we laughed, we all apologized because we knew that we had caused her pain in exchange for our delight and humor. (We had also wanted to teach her to stop sucking her thumb.) I again was yelled at by my mother, I was put on a time-out, and I couldn't play with my cousins for two days.

As tiger cubs, we are expected to apologize for just about everything, regardless of whether we're aware of our missteps. Essentially, these are apologies to admit wrongdoings that may or may not have occurred and/or to make a person feel better. But, most importantly, these apologies are meant to acknowledge the authority in the room, which is most often our tiger moms. Call it the non-apology.

To this day, I'm still not always sure why I'm apologizing for many of my actions. Sometimes, it's because I think I've inadvertently caused pain to another person; but many times, I find myself apologizing for things that I don't have to apologize for.

I apologize if a person doesn't feel well.

I apologize for being late.

I apologize if a meeting runs long.

I apologize if I can't meet a person because I have a scheduling conflict.

I apologize if I don't make a deadline.

I apologize to my vendors or my 1099 contractors if I pay my bills a few days late.

I apologize for making someone feel bad.

Apologizing is ingrained in the tiger cub. This is something that most Asian Americans do because it's a form of respect and deference. And it's a habit I'm working on breaking.

7. Ensure your cubs perform to the best of their ability. And ensure your cubs keep up their performances. They are reflections of you.

For many tiger cubs, performing is a key part of growing up. Sabrina and I were made to perform for our aunties and other relatives, and the pressure was always immense. We were walking billboards for our parents' investments in our studies in music, athletics, arts, linguistics, and sciences. Our performances and our grades—straight As or A+s—were testaments to how rich we were, and they proved that we could succeed in the Asian way, that we would become functioning adults when we got older. Giving a perfect performance and being obedient to our parents (regardless of what their request might be) made them look like good parents to their friends.

While this description might seem like a gross exaggeration in the eyes of non-Asians, this was simply the reality we lived with. Take Alan, for example. We shared a music stand in the California Youth Symphony orchestra. Alan was a fellow tiger cub, and the pressure to perform became so intense that he ended up at Stanford Hospital's psychiatric ward for over three months. He had been programmed to perform excellently every time, and under that pressure, he hid his true feelings of what he wanted. I learned later that Alan had quit Palo Alto High School and had gone to a facility in Germany to seek treatment after being at Stanford's psychiatric ward—and the clincher was that he'd left without the blessing from his parents. He had learned about the German facility from his "big brother" at his Chinese school. Alan's big brother was an older "recovered" tiger-parented child who swore by the treatment in Germany. He was in his final year at Stanford University and had just gotten a job at a hedge fund in Silicon Valley on his own terms. Inspired by this example, Alan scraped up his money and flew to Germany. The psychologists at that facility likened Alan's tiger-parented experience to that of a prisoner of war with PTSD, and they treated him with the same medications they would give for that diagnosis.

After two years of treatment and therapy at the German facility, Alan recovered—with not just his soul but with his true purpose intact. He was considered healed enough to return to society, and he ultimately attended the University of California, Berkeley, graduating with honors in the science department and going on to become an engineer at Intel. He never really shared much about the years during his breakdown, except the brief details that have been described above. Still, Alan's story is a shining example of the possibility of another path. Tiger cubs are taught that if we perform—if we are positive reflections of our parents—we will succeed in life. Although Alan's parents were unsure what his life's trajectory would be when he left home, he's proven that he could be successful despite breaking this rule.

These are the known, unwritten rules of the tiger household. And, theoretically, they're easy to navigate when you have firm boundaries, like a school schedule or the home schedule my mom created for me and Sabrina. But the rules that we don't talk about—the ones that we don't even know about—are the ones that are trickiest.

These are the rules where, even if you think you are doing the right thing, you are still wrong. In fact, no matter what you do, no matter how much you try to please your family, you lose. You get publicly shamed in front of your aunties or experience the displeasure of your parents. You are essentially wrong, no matter what. Because of an action done or not done, because you didn't show up in a particular way to your tiger parent, or because of some comment you may or may not have made that didn't meet your mom's expectation of the way things "should" have been. Now, that's the zinger: the game of whack-a-mole that drives you crazy, and you don't even know the rules of the game…

When my sister and I were growing up, our mother held us up to a set of unspoken expectations that we didn't know about. She never speak about these rules, yet we were supposed to abide by them. If we didn't meet her expectations, she felt hard done by, and it was hard for me and my sister to experience our mom's disappointment, disapproval, and unkind words in response. I was an inquisitive, curious child, and I tried to understand the boundaries; I tried to learn about life and get to know people. But sometimes the tiger-parenting style—with its unpredictable, unspoken rules—got the best of me; it tempered my spirit and my inquisitive nature to learn more, ask more questions, and speak up. Two incidents in particular exemplify what I'm talking about.

When my mom was teaching at her middle school, she had a good friend named Casey. Casey was an avid diver, and he started dropping off abalone, crab, and shrimp for us. He was an elderly man with gray hair; he was five feet ten inches tall, with a thick build. and a sweet personality. It seemed like he really cared for my mother and us.

Whenever he went diving, we'd get the call, and I'd hear my mother coo, "Yes, Casey, how nice!" into the phone receiver. "Kids, we're having abalone tonight!" she'd yell out happily to us. She'd then primp in the mirror and put on makeup.

About twenty minutes later, there would be a ring from the doorbell, typically around the dinner hour. Casey would be standing there in his full slick, black diving suit, and he'd drop off enough shrimp or abalone to feed all four of us for two meals.

One time, when he rang the doorbell, I answered it and called for my mother.

"Did you bring crab, shrimp, or abalone?" I expectantly asked him. I was excited for our seafood dinner. I was eight at the time.

Casey looked at me and smiled with a wistful look in his eyes, like he wasn't used to being around children or didn't have children of his own. "I brought five crab this time. Victoria, or is it Sabrina?"

"Victoria." I gingerly smiled. "Do you have kids?"

A shadow crossed Casey's face as though I had asked him about a ghost. Of course, it was at that moment when my mother came, and she scolded me to never ask questions like that. It was inappropriate.

"I apologize for my daughter," she said to her friend, flustered that she hadn't answered the door. She pushed past me and held me tightly behind her, pinching me in the process.

"Ouch! Mom, you're hurting me," I said. I wriggled in pain as my mom clung to my arm, pinching me the entire time.

"Casey, I'm so sorry. Victoria is just so rude and difficult. You know, eight-year-olds." She laughed that awful hollow laugh, the one that sounds fake and forced.

Mom had my arm pinned, so I knew that I was in trouble. "Thank you so much for the crab," she said to Casey.

They chitchatted a bit and then said their goodbyes. Finally, she shut the door, letting go of me as the door closed.

"Mom, why are you wearing lipstick? And why did you do that to me?" I asked curiously. My arm hurt. I looked down at where my mother had pinched me, and I saw a giant red mark beginning to grow.

"I told you never to ask questions like that. It's rude," she said.

I was confused. She had never talked to me about asking such questions. "I was trying to make conversation."

"Victoria, you are wrong. Let's go the bathroom. You've got to learn what's right and wrong."

I tried holding my ground. "You've said so many times that it's rude not to make conversation. That it's rude to sit there. And now it's rude to make conversation?" Confusion filled my face, mixed with the hope that my mother might empathize with my dilemma of making conversation, that she might let me off the hook for something I had theoretically got "wrong."

"Let's go, young lady," my mom said.

She dragged me by my hair from the front door and down the long, narrow hallway to the pink bathroom. She grabbed the white step stool that we had bought from Macy's, and she had me stand at the sink while she washed out my mouth. This was one time out of many when I would get my mouth washed out with her favorite bar of soap. I had gotten my mouth washed out so many times that I'd lost count over the years.

This one act compounded on many of the other ways that my mom's tiger parenting was geared to control and guide her young. This incident showed me that there's a wrong way to ask questions and there's a line of inappropriateness that one should never cross. But it all remained so murky and undefined. What were the "right" and "wrong" questions? Where was that line?

Another whack-a-mole incident happened was when I was in my sophomore year of high school. My father typically drove me to school, but on this particular day, my mother took me. Typically, it was a fifteen-minute drive through suburban Millbrae and Burlingame to Aragon High School, which was nestled high in the hills of San Mateo. But, on this morning, it turned out to be a forty-five-minute affair.

My mother was upset at my father because he had just lost his driver's license due to a speeding ticket. This, in turn, had effectively canceled my mother and father's joint insurance policy. So my mother begrudgingly had to take me to school.

She was on a particular tear that day. I had tuned her out as I often did when she went on her rampages, cussing my dad out: "Your dad is no good for anything. He's selfish. He doesn't understand finances. We can't rely on him. He's no good. I can't believe he lost his license. Because of this, I'm on my own."

Normally, I wouldn't have spoken up, but as we sped out of Millbrae, I noticed that somehow we were no longer driving in the right direction toward my school.

"Mom, um, where are we going?" I asked as we whizzed up Larkspur Drive to the 280—not the usual El Camino or 101 South that my dad took to avoid early-morning traffic.

"How dare you question me? Who do you think you are? You are just like your dad," she yelled at me.

"You aren't driving in the right direction," I said.

My mom turned on me. "What an ungrateful child. I didn't raise you to question me. I'm trying to give you the best, giving you all the finest things. I have given you so much criticism to help you, and you still haven't learned right from wrong. You just don't trust me, and I'm doing my best for you…"

Mom would often feel hard done by our actions, my dad's actions, life, or the path she had chosen. She'd bob and veer, guided by the tiger-parent principles that she needed to instill in us, while adding a layer of harshness due to her feeling overwhelmed by life. I wasn't sure if other tiger-parented cubs experienced what I was going through—trying to navigate between saying and doing things that my mother would deem inappropriate—but as I got older and started talking to other tiger cubs more openly, I saw that their experiences were indeed similar, although in varying forms and flavors.

I stared out the window, deciding to say nothing at all because, if I did, there would be a harsh reaction and repercussions from me speaking up. So I chose not to say anything at all. We were heading north on 280, in the opposite direction of school, passing through the San Bruno fog and the green topography, heading toward her school. My mom was talking about me to me, but all I heard was *Wha, wha, wha* in the background.

We were about two blocks from her school when she finally noticed where we were.

"Victoria, why didn't you stop me from going to my school? Why didn't you say something?" she asked.

"I tried, but you didn't listen," I said.

Somehow, my mother's voice got louder and angrier, like a blaring foghorn less than five feet away from my ears.

"This is your fault. You always make things so difficult for everyone. You should have said something. What were you thinking? Now we're both going to be late," she said angrily.

After that, I learned to hold my tongue and not say anything. I learned to walk on pins and needles. It was like playing Pac-Man: I was walking through a maze, eating pellets that would make me grow strong, and then I'd eat one pellet, and I'd inexplicably shrink again and have to course-correct until I reached my goal. Except, with my mother, I'd never reach the goal. I never felt like I was being heard—truly heard—because when I did speak up, I was told that I was being difficult or that I was a problem, a nuisance. I could never do the right thing, because the one woman I adored—whom I desperately wanted to please—was never proud of me, or so I thought.

These unspoken—and often contradictory—rules taught me later in life to stay in the box, to hold my tongue, to not speak out or get to know people as deeply as I could. Today, I'm sometimes likened to Spock from *Star Trek* because I'm so adept at compartmentalizing my feelings and only making them available in certain scenarios to reflect whichever scene I'm in.

Tips for the Tiger Cub

Tips to Unravel the Unspoken Rules

Have you ever found yourself experiencing anxiety around your parents, and/or do you live in fear of when the next pin is going to drop? I have. Several exercises have helped me get through the stressful moments when I'm faced with overwhelm or anxiety around my parents:

1. When faced with a particularly daunting experience with your tiger mother, take a deep breath and look at the stressful situation with objective eyes, knowing that your mother picked up the trait from one of her loved ones or a previously traumatic event. Ask yourself: What is she reacting to? Why did she react in the way that she did? Where did the pattern come from? By reflecting and analyzing the situation, you'll then be able to understand what runs your mother.

2. **The Elevator Exercise:** Close your eyes. Take a deep breath, and then imagine an elevator moving up your body, from your feet to the top of your head, and then down again past your feet and through the ground. Do this two or three times while deeply breathing. Then open your eyes. See if your perspective has changed. Mine always does.
3. **Get your calm back by resetting your thymus** (the gland between your breastbones that helps with normalizing stress). Make a fist and grind into your breastbone clockwise and counterclockwise. If this is too much for you, try thymus tapping (i.e. tapping on your thymus with two to three fingers) three times a day for twenty seconds. Both movements activate the thymus gland that is responsible for T cell production and boosting your immune system. (This is a useful grounding technique.) There's also a "reset button" one inch beneath your belly button. Do the same, pressing one or two inches deep into your abdomen.
4. Journal about three or four times when you've faced your tiger mom's unspoken rules while growing up. Think about incidents when you were punished for something you said or did (or didn't say or didn't do). How did you feel? Where have you carried that feeling forward in your life? How has it served you or not served you? Is that pattern serving you now? If it's not serving you now, call attention to it and be aware of it.

CHAPTER 2

In the Eyes of a Tiger Cub

BEING RAISED BY A tiger mom is a unique experience. We tiger cubs are faced with a set of rules and expectations that are intended to prepare us for weathering life's up and downs. And while this parenting style does instill certain strengths, it also bombards us with challenges that most non-Asians never have to face.

Resilience is born by tiger parenting through critical comments, rigid structure, and the like. While these items may seem benign on the surface, it weighs on the child—these rules that one must follow as a tiger cub. Like a load of bricks, this duty sits upon your shoulders—and eventually, the weight of it can start to crush you. Unlike the outlier tiger-parented child who was caned or slapped, or known as the black sheep and ridiculed when they disobeyed, my twin sister and I were raised in a typical tiger-parented environment: we were held to a strict schedule, and we were yelled at or spanked when we fell out of line, couldn't follow the rules, or did not pay heed to our aunties. We generally held our tongues when asked for our opinions—because if we had opinions that differed from our parents', well, that was just not acceptable. For most people, this doesn't sound so bad—but for my sister and me (and for many other tiger cubs I've spoken to), it was.

How bad can a tiger mom be to your brain and mental well-being? Think about it this way: You're at the top of your game; maybe you are the solo violinist at the Boston Symphony, maybe you are the valedictorian in your high school class, or maybe you are a doctor who has successfully performed their first open-heart surgery. And yet your mom finds one flaw in your accomplishment, one minor detail that she believes would have made all the difference in the world. For the violinist, it's that one note. For the valedictorian, it's that one A-. And for the heart surgeon, it's that one suture that could have been "perfect." That "flaw" is pointed out to you, loud and clear—and although you've outperformed 99 percent of your peers, that flaw is amplified by your mom to all of your closest aunties and uncles.

It's this kind of soul-crushing experience that pushes us tiger cubs to perform that much more, to be that much better, because we are wracked with guilt that we didn't perform to the best of our abilities and that we've somehow disappointed not only our mom but our entire family. The thing is, your mom thinks that she's "helping" and being a good mom when she does this; in her eyes, she's providing constructive feedback and nitpicking out of her form of "love."

That is the epitome of a tiger mom.

In the Eyes of a Tiger Cub

Growing up, I knew my mother loved me and was preparing me for a functioning role in society where I could enjoy financial security and commercial success. But I also needed to adhere to the bounds of Asian tiger society—and the pressure not to deviate is immense. Like dutiful tiger cubs everywhere, I put aside my happiness and hustled to be accomplished and meet my tiger mom's expectations. I knew that this reflected well on my family, and I had grown up trying to be the tiger mom's dream. In the process, I tried so hard to excel at everything that I just became a jack-of-all-trades and master of none. My mom pushed me to excel in so many things that I never knew what I was a master of. (And this is something I am still trying to discover as an adult.) Most tiger-parented cubs are known for doing so many things (I was known for playing the viola, playing the flute, singing in choir, being on the track team and the cross-country team, being on the student council, and being on the honor roll), but this multitasking and being good at everything is only OK until you need to be *great* at one thing. In fact, most tiger cubs can outdo pretty much any other ethnicity in terms of activity, but when it comes to standing out on one thing, well, that's where we fail—and fail big.

There is also a level of desensitization that tiger moms instill in their cubs to ensure they can succeed. This desensitization comes about because the tiger mom loves her young so much that she'll try many approaches to build their self-esteem and help them adjust well to society. Going through the experience of being tiger-parented can be traumatizing and can lead to many scars and anger. But knowing that your mom's actions were a form of love (or even a love language) can heal the wounds a little.

And it's amazing to see how that desensitization can benefit us in times of turmoil, like during the COVID-19 pandemic. My tiger grandmother and mom had experienced so much turmoil in their lives (especially as women), and during those times, they had to keep going to survive. So, when I was faced with a similar situation, as their tiger cub, I also had to keep going instead of cowering in the corner. This dynamic is very similar to what we see in animal behavior. Ultimately, the tiger mom is expressing a form of love by helping her cubs learn to the survive in the world. Consider this form of love as conditioning that is inspired by Mother Nature. All animals raise their young to survive in the wild, fiercely protecting their young and coddling them for the first few months as they start to learn and grow. And then the mother transitions the young, testing their instinctive survival skills. For example, mother grizzly bears find food for their young for the first few months, and then they teach their young to hunt for salmon in lakes and streams. Ultimately, it's up to the cub to learn how to hunt and find its own food. The mother weans the cub, knowing instinctively that the cub will make it in the wild—and, if not, it's up to Mother Nature to weed out those who underperform. Asian tiger cubs are conditioned similarly. For many years, I likened being raised by my Asian tiger mom to being raised in a prison—a beautiful one where the warden allowed me to pick out the interior decor, but where the warden would get the final say on what that prison looked like, what my schedule looked like, and what I could do within those prison walls. While I could pick out the color of my walls, the bedspread, and my clothes, if I wanted to explore outside of the prison walls, there was a metaphorical electric fence that would shock me back into my prison and back into submission—a "desensitivity" training, so to speak.

Through our tiger mom's harshness and rules, we're taught to fend for ourselves, because the elements around us tend to be harsher. (For example, fitting into peer groups, being in a competitive work environment, or maybe even facing inadvertent discrimination in areas like going for a top managerial position, competing for a scholarship, or trying to become a partner at a professional services firm.) To some degree, our tiger mothers push us to the breaking point so that they can see us survive. And, for the most part, the strong-minded learn to survive even the toughest situations. During COVID, I remembered a story my aunt once told me when I was complaining about my mother and grandmother. She said that some mothers are like eagles who build their nests high in the mountains. When the baby eagles are young, the mother eagle trains them to fly by pushing them off the cliff. She would save the babies right before they landed on the ground, and she'd keep doing that until the babies learned to fly. Compare this to a mother chicken, who is too protective of her baby chicks. I don't think I would ever mirror the chicken's style of parenting, but knowing that my mom was pushing me hard (albeit sometimes too hard) so I could fly does provide some comfort.

A friend of mine shared a story about a time when she had met a Chinese immigrant while she was shopping in Costco. The man was trying to find items on his grocery list and had asked an employee where certain goods were. He was having difficulty with his translations because his Google translation app wasn't working well, and the employee was frustrated at the man because he didn't speak English and didn't know how to communicate. Luckily, my friend came over and translated for the man, but she also recommended to him that he learn English, or he would be ostracized by his Chinese community. The man thanked her, and he explained that he had recently immigrated to the US after being prosecuted for something the government believed he had done in China. He had been a doctor in China, but because he had fled without a good means of living nor a valid US medical license, he now found himself working two menial jobs and taking English classes at night so that he could fit into the US. This man was facing steep challenges every day, and yet he continued to take steps to improve his situation. That's resilience. That's what it means to be raised by a tiger mom.

Being raised by an Asian tiger mom primes you for resilience later in life. Think about it: while other children were being coddled, were looked after more, and had more free time than we did, our tiger moms had us on strict regimens that would have been fit for a soldier in military camp. Yes, we might have moaned to our friends and loved ones about being dragged to our Advanced Placement classes, to our piano or violin lessons, to our Chinese lessons, and to all our other extracurricular activities while also having to study two to three hours each night to get our straight As so that we didn't embarrass our parents. But that dedication, rigor, and structure that our tiger moms provided helped us; and it's still helping us to this day as we have to keep routines. In bad times and good times, we don't have to think about keeping ourselves organized, because ingrained within us is the need to adhere to a fixed schedule.

In a twisted way, those disapproving stares by our moms—just like a quick tap on the head or a roar by the mama bear—were actually a form of love. The judgmental looks of disdain helped us to quickly get back in line, and the harsh words were a form of advice that meant they loved us. They helped us to constantly realize that we needed to do better and perform better than the rest, and they provided us with the motivation needed to succeed in spite of the uncertainty and negativity of our American environment.

Because our tiger moms wanted us to succeed, they found the time to criticize us in the first place. Theoretically, their criticism prepared us for functioning roles in society. And, in the harshest of circumstances during COVID, we tiger cubs were not staring at the TV in horror and waiting for the stock market or the unemployment numbers to rise and fall. Instead, those moments became light-bulb moments, and we found ourselves saying this such as, "Wait! This is familiar to me. All of you can fail, but I know I'm not going to." We asked our fellow tiger cubs, "How much did you make in the stock market?" or, "Did you get an increase in pay?" or, "Have you gotten funding for your start-up yet?" We were pushing ourselves—and each other—to succeed.

When faced with Asian guilt, many of us have tried to repress it when we were growing up. But, as adults, it becomes an asset during the hard times—like during COVID, or an economic recession, or a job loss, or immigrating to another country. Because of our rigorous upbringing, it's a relief that we can endure whatever hardships are thrown at us—however hard they may be—while others may not be able to survive. That said, we feel guilty because we know that we can survive while others may not have the same type of resiliency skills as we do. That guilt allows us to feel empathy toward others who have lost their jobs, can't seem to figure out how to pivot to be self-sufficient, or are paralyzed with fear after almost five months of lockdown. That Asian guilt—that sinking feeling that tugs at your heartstrings because you know you aren't doing something that meets your mom's or aunties' approval—has helped you show up in this world to be a functioning adult, to find creativity and do what is necessary to feed your children, and to come up with strategies so that you're living a really good life on the other side. Think about it: Were you able to buckle down and really use COVID for your advantage? How did you perform in the face of that adversity? After COVID, I talked with other Asian tiger cubs about their routines during that time. For example, my esthetician, a tiger-parented child, developed an online wellness course with her friend (another tiger-parented child) to keep both of them positive, focused, and motivated—and, most importantly, it kept food on their tables. As an added benefit, their course helped others, too.

What's even more inspiring is that she and her friend are still working on creating other ways of making money by offering wellness products, beauty products, and more in their online store. In another example, my acupuncturist, another Asian tiger-reared cub, created virtual office hours to cover wellness routines with her clients during lockdown, and she finished writing a book that will be published shortly. For me, I was able to complete a new house build in the middle of COVID while simultaneously pursuing a lawsuit because one of my contractors had run off with my money. I also gave a TEDx Talk in 2020, and I pivoted and grew my business. Even in the face of adversity, I've been resilient, which my mother's love conditioned me to do. I have talked with other tiger-parented cubs who focused on work and their home lives during COVID, and it was business as usual for them, too.

While this type of parenting may be great for times when you need resiliency, for everyday living it becomes hard because life is not always a fight-or-flight experience. Life is a *being* experience, a time to be aware of the present, not live in the future. It's about being aware of your surroundings in the now rather than always worrying, stressing, and planning for the future of who you want to be, who you will dare to be, who you will become.

At some point, if your soul isn't strong enough—if you can't take all the negative criticism, the nitpicking, and being told that you aren't good enough—you crack, you develop bad habits, or you may even end up in the psychiatric ward, like my friend Alan (see chapter 1). I was one of the lucky ones. Unlike Alan, I didn't crack early in life, but being tiger-parented has taken its toll on me in some serious ways that have impacted my relationships, my business life, and my overall financial health. It actually might have been better if I had cracked earlier in life because I might have started to make my own choices sooner.

When you see Asians on TV (except in comedies, where they are expected to be silly), they are portrayed with typical Asian characteristics: the aggressiveness, the seriousness, the competitiveness, the heightened state of expecting that things will go wrong, and the inability to relax. This is really typical of the Asian culture, with some exceptions (primarily those who were not raised in tiger-parented households). In fact, it's rare to see an Asian smile, easily share their emotions, or be personable, because these behaviors are just not cultural norms. (You may be asking about my mom's Filipino side. In Filipino culture, everyone seems happy and personable, but let me tell you: that comes with a price. It has been my experience with my Filipino friends and family that there is a huge amount of love and camaraderie that exists alongside fierce competition and suppression of people's true feelings because it's not polite to air grievances or flaws in public.)

While my aggressiveness, seriousness, competitiveness, and detachment have always been strong, my ability to make solid decisions about men, business, and otherwise was poor—primarily because I cared so much about what my tiger mom wanted. The result was that I was reverse-wired by Asian tiger parenting. You couldn't tell me, "Good job!" or, "That's an amazing speech," or, "You are kind and generous." I'd only get suspicious. That switch had been shut off a number of years ago. In fact, I responded better to criticism, negative feedback, and adversity than positive feedback. "You could do better by…" or, "You said 'Houston' incorrectly," or…the list goes on. Growing up, this type of response always pushed me to do better, be better, and strive to be the best at what I did. Later, in college, I always got A+s. And I was so used to my mother's criticism as a form of love that I didn't question what the impact would be as I got older—to the relationships that I would have, the friendships that I would form, or the work that I would do. I didn't know any better. Three cases clearly exemplify how these traits impacted the people around me and my decisions on who I would become.

It's said that you unconsciously tell people how to treat you. Or you've probably heard the expression that you attract who you are. When I was in my early twenties, I had become so desensitized to the point that I put myself in what American standards would call an abusive relationship. Peter was handsome and creative, I'll give him that, but he was also one of the worst souls a person could touch. Throughout our relationship of over eight years, whenever Peter was angry, he would say to me, "You fucking bitch," "You cunt," or, "You are stupid." Oftentimes, at Christmas, he would tell me that I didn't deserve a gift, so I would buy my own gifts and would stick them under the tree so that I would have something to open on Christmas morning. And, while he never did hit me, he punched holes in walls, he hit our neighbor's cars on the street, and he even smashed the windows of the neighbor's house…just because.

I tolerated Peter's behavior because I thought it was a form of love. Growing up in a tiger-parented household, I had become used to the harshness of this reality. While my mother didn't scream expletives at me, I endured her harsh words and being told that I wasn't good enough. Unlike with Peter, I knew my mom did the tug of guilt and said negative words to push me to succeed; I knew it was done out of love, in the only way she knew how.

Being tiger-parented grooms you to experience the extremes of the harshness of life. However, this type of environment enabled me to choose the monster that I eventually married, because I was so familiar with tolerating harshness. So, for eight years, I braced myself for my heart to break yet again, which happened too many times as the years went on. I didn't know I could choose something else; I didn't know that there was anything different, that I could actually make a choice to say no…until I was on the phone with my mom one day.

"Mom, how's Uncle Reynold?" I asked.

"He got divorced from Teresa. Terrible news."

"What?" I replied, in shock.

"He got divorced. And he's happy."

"You are OK with his divorce?" I asked.

"Good for him," my mother said. "He seems happier divorced. It's a shame, though, because we can no longer do activities as a foursome."

From that conversation, I discerned that, while my mother was disappointed by the loss of the social aspects of having another couple to dine or travel with, she felt that the stain of divorce wasn't as big of an issue as I had blown it up to be in my mind.

Within several weeks of that conversation, I had thrown Peter out of the house. And a year after that conversation, I was divorced. Because I had been shown that there was a different way. Because my mom had deemed that it was acceptable to get divorced. That's the power of the Asan tiger mom.

After I had divorced Peter, I found myself in a relationship with someone I never thought I would fall in love with. When I was with him, the grass was always greener, the sky was always brighter. In fact, we would laugh like hyenas whenever we were together. But my desensitization was so extreme that Liam couldn't handle it. He would give me compliments and would do something nice for me, and I would downplay whatever he did, to the point where it was no longer a joy for him to do those things for me. We would make meals, and I would inadvertently cut him off when he talked, I'd yell at him, or I'd prevent him from helping me. Emotionally, I was shut down to the point where I forgot that I had a partner. For example, there were times when we were supposed to go to the symphony or to a show, and I would get a phone call from him because I had forgotten to pick him up on my way to the symphony. We ultimately broke up because his tender heart couldn't take it. He said, "Victoria, I can't be with you; you want to be treated so badly., and I can't do that to you. I'm not that kind of person." He tried to break through the harshness that I had experienced from my childhood and from my marriage with Peter, but he ultimately could not succeed in his quest. It was only then that I realized that I had to make a different choice in how I interacted with my environment and how I responded to men and to other people. I had to break free from the desensitization.

After my relationship with Liam, I realized that I wanted to be a better person. I started to see that the world wasn't full of harsh word; that I could exist, even if I wasn't pushed, even if I didn't have to perform. I could just be myself. However, I didn't get this memo until later in life at the ripe old age of thirty-six.

As in my personal life, there have also been occasions in my work life when this desensitization has caused my sharp tongue (or my sharp words in written form) to get me into trouble. In fact, my team at work called me Cuddly Bear because my words could be inadvertently harsh, without a filter of consideration for how they would affect the other person.

Carrie, one of my media relations pitchers, had worked for me for almost four years, and she used to be upset at me all the time. I didn't know how she felt—until two years into the job, during a weekly one-on-one meeting, when she brought me a bunch of printed emails that I had written to her.

"Victoria, I can't take it anymore," she said.

"What?" I asked.

"You write edits to each of my pitches, and you basically want me to rewrite the entire pitch. Am I not a good writer? I'm damn good at what I do. Our clients get really good results. Should I be searching for another job?"

"Huh?" I asked, confused. "What are you talking about?"

She threw the emails at me. There must have been at least thirty pages of corrections and rewrites that I had made to her initial pitches.

"You don't like what I do. I've never heard you say, 'Good job,' or, 'That's great,' on any of the coverage that we get for our clients. All I hear is critical feedback. And I'm done. I want to know that I'm doing a good job, or I can't work for you anymore."

We both stood up, Carrie towering above me by twelve inches. And, at that moment, after being presented with the stack of printed emails, I realized that she was right. I had not given her praise at all. I had just doled out feedback—what she interpreted as criticism—because that was what I had known from growing up with a tiger mom.

So, as we stood, I grabbed for her and hugged her. "Carrie, you are doing a terrific job. If you weren't, you wouldn't be here."

"Such encouraging words, Boss-Lady," she said, laughing wholeheartedly as she realized that I was trying to be encouraging.

"Carrie, I'll try harder to let you know of my appreciation and to recognize your good work. But you let me know when I'm being harsh, OK? I don't recognize it. I really am a cuddly bear," I said.

"Cuddly Bear! I'm going to call you that every time, so you know when you are being harsh!" She laughed.

And, with that, she walked out of my office, instantaneously happier. All she had wanted was praise, recognition for her good work, that attaboy. I realized that I could not remember hearing a single attaboy from my mother when I was growing up. It was always a critical word or disapproval of some sort.

Making good work decisions was also hard because I was still faced with the pressure to look good. About five years ago, I was waiting to complete the sale of the organization that I had built over the last ten years. Both deals fell through because I didn't make the right moves; I didn't make the right choices for me. The first deal was a bit sloppy. My organization had a net profitability of 39 percent at the time, with some of its offices operating in the red. I, however, was gung ho to merge, because of my need to appear successful and accomplished. I saw that the buyer's mindset was the same; they came from a similar culture and had similar personalities. They used big thinking, and I just liked them. They, like my organization, were scrappy and fun. I merged some of our accounts with little, if any, paperwork to integrate our people. We, in fact, were paying them. The deal ultimately fell through when the buyer's partner (who was handling the deal) was fired. Our merger/acquisition got put on the back burner.

The second deal was with a much more polished organization. The buyer was ready to do the deal, and it should have been a quick sale. But there were several caveats: Because I had been in the midst of a transition/transaction, our revenue wasn't as high as in the previous year, so we were not ready. We also had resigned a few accounts and had turned over people with the anticipation of merging staff. I took my eyes off of the ball, and the deal fell through. The last half of the year was spent revamping the organization and picking up the pieces to create something that could scale. As I got ready to hand over the business once again, that deal also fell through. At the end of the day, the acquiring company found that our organizations were not aligned, and they decided that we should hold off and continue our referral relationship. This was not something that I had been prepared for.

For me, this was where my tiger cub instinct kicked in as I tried to block my failures from my purview. The people around me knew that I had been preparing the organization for sale—it was hard not to, as I had talked about it and prepared for it for eighteen months. I had been excited to work with a larger team; and, to some degree, I had gone through a series of staff changes to prep the books. And when the acquiring company said they wanted to hold off, my first thoughts were, *What will people think? What do I tell people?* Waves of humiliation from other people's judgments washed over me. *What do I do now? Where do I go? What do I want?* I needed a navigation system to point me to where I needed to go, where I wanted to go. This Asian thing about shame—shame from my aunties, shame from my parents, shame from my sister—sat on my shoulders as I experienced waves of disappointment and sadness. I kicked myself for having told people—a lot of people—about what I was doing. I'd told them about the struggles I had gone through, the contracts that I had won to grow the organization, and the pressure that I had put on myself to be a role model. I was confronting all the traits that I had learned from my tiger mom. I didn't want to go back to my mother or my family and tell them that both sales had fallen through. I thought of all the time I had spent chasing a fleeting dream, only to find it crushed. It represented a larger vision that I saw for myself in this lifetime.

I couldn't tell myself, *Victoria, it's OK. Let's look on the bright side of things. Look at the things that it has allowed you to build, to explore.* Instead, I felt that I had been humiliated; I had lost my dreams, and I knew that I could have done better. It was a pattern that I had experienced time and time again since my childhood. Good could have been better; there could have been a more predictable outcome, a winnable outcome. I could have won over the acquiring company's team with my personality, with my team, with our strategy. If we had won those accounts.

I couldn't see the beauty and freedom in that moment, with the gifts that I had, with the thriving organization that could scale. It was here that I could have parked the voice of my inner tiger mom at the door. I could have said to myself, *Hey, now you can scale. You can do what you need to do. You can work with a good leadership/business coach. You can find new revenue sources. You have the freedom to build whatever organization you want. And you can recoup the money that you invested in the business by rapidly scaling the business.* I so desperately needed that pep talk, but I was afraid to ask for it.

I couldn't admit that I needed to ask for help, because that wasn't what I had been taught to do. But it's human to do so. We can't always have a brave face in these situations. We all need and want a pep talk from time to time. We all need someone to tell us the truth of who we are. And that's what the tiger mom prevents us from doing. We can't ask for help, because it's admitting defeat. We can't ask for love or show vulnerability to anyone. Because, if we do, well, we aren't succeeding.

These instances were life-defining, primarily because I finally saw that I had been running the patterns that I'd learned when I was young. Despite each of these different situations telling me one thing, my inner programming defined the moment and the events that occurred. It was as if I didn't have a choice. My past prevented me from seeing the present; it kept me from living in the moment and seeing what was around me. In my personal life and my work life, I had been so programmed to get through it, to go for the goal, or to forge ahead and succeed, and I missed the subtleties of life, the clues to actually living. In the case of my marriage, there were clues that could have told me that Peter truly was a bad man, and that I had the choice to be in a different relationship. With Carrie, I didn't see that she needed positive reinforcement to succeed at work. And in both instances of the acquisitions, I missed the red flags that the mergers would not have been good for me or my organization. For me to change and start seeing thing differently, something—anything—needed to bop me on the head and say, *Hey, Victoria. Wake up! I'm screaming at you. NOW.*

I'm not the only tiger cub who has faced this kind of struggle. We get so stuck in our patterns that we miss seeing the sunset or hearing the laughter of our friends, because we are the ones who are still working or in study hall. Think about it. When have you ever smiled just for the sake of smiling, from pure joy, without worrying that something will dampen your happiness? When have you done something nice for someone without expecting something in return? For the most part, it's as if we Asian Americans go through the motions of life, doing the activities we do, because we are expected to, without any thought of disregarding what our parents want and who they want us to be.

One of my friends, who is Asian but was not raised in a tiger-parent household, sees the true grip of how this parenting style impacts teenagers and young adults. She counsels first-generation and second-generation Asian children who are so critical and fearful of their choices for college majors because they feel that if they make a wrong decision or don't get an A or don't graduate, they'll bring shame to their families. So they go through mental anguish, afraid to talk with their peers or their family about the internal struggles they face. My friend's fear is that these kids' goals and their inner critics (their parents) will lead them toward suicide or unrest when they graduate from college and are on their own in the real world. While she's trying to help them by equipping them with techniques and strategies to get them out of their heads, she realizes that, before the kids can change and see anything differently, they need to be present and appreciate what they have—and they need to realize that their parents' goals and their parents' values don't run their lives.

It's hard to make that shift to start differentiating your parents' goals and values from your own. You are a blank canvas. But the only way to understand this is to understand yourself as you are today, not as your future self. Until you understand who you are today, your parents' values, dreams, and culture will continue to define your future.

Tips for the Tiger Cub

TIPS ON UNWINDING FROM THE GRIPS OF THE ASIAN TIGER MOM
Gather three blank pages.
1. On the first page, draw a vertical line down the middle of the page. On one side of the page, write down as a header, "My Parents' Values." On the other side, write down as a header, "My Values." Spend at least five minutes journaling on each. What did you learn? What are your values? Where did you learn your values? What defines your values?
2. On the second page, draw a vertical line down the middle of the page. On one side of the page, write down as a header, "My Parents' Dreams." On the other side, write down as a header, "My Dreams." What type of person did your parents want you to be? What profession did they want you to be in? Think back to when you were young. Who did you want to be? What do you want to do? What would you do if you felt free from the bonds of your parents to do the things that you want?
3. On the third page, draw a vertical line down the middle of the page. On one side of the page, write down all of your critical internal sayings. Spend five to ten minutes on this. On the other side of the page, write down where each saying came from. Did

it come from your mother? Father? Aunt? Uncle? Grandmother? School teacher? Next to each saying, also write the opposite (positive) expression. (We need to negate the negative.) If you do this every day for a week, you'll be surprised at what comes up.

CHAPTER 3

Finding Freedom from Control

FOR A TIGER MOM to instill the desired traits and values in her cub, she has an incredibly effective tool: control. All of those rules, expectations, and conditioning we've been talking about only work because Mom keeps a firm hold on every aspect of her cub's life. And this dynamic inevitably fosters a codependent relationship.

According to the American Mental Health Institute, "Codependency is a learned behavior that can be passed down from one generation to another. It is an emotional and behavioral condition that affects an individual's ability to have a healthy, mutually satisfying relationship. It is also known as "relationship addiction" because people with codependency often form or maintain relationships that are one-sided, emotionally destructive and/or abusive."[2] Among the traits that the American Mental Health Institute identifies as codependent are: a sense of guilt when asserting oneself, an unhealthy dependence on others, an extreme need for approval and recognition, lack of trust in self and others, a tendency to do more than their share all the time, and a tendency to be hurt when people don't recognize their efforts.

Yes, there are dozens of questionnaires on the internet that you can take to determine if you are codependent. But that's not the point—you probably already identified codependency in your family dynamic when you read the previous paragraph. In fact, my point in raising this issue is to help you see that your own thoughts, ideas, and dreams of who you want to become should theoretically come from you and should be supported by your parents; your parents should not suppress them as fantasies or tell you that you shouldn't follow your dreams. As tiger-parented cubs, our ideas of who we are and who we've become—because of how we were raised—are directly attributed to our parents' dreams, values and images of who they want us to be. We can dream about what our non-Asian American peers have: parents who support their child's dreams, traits, and who they are; parents who accept and nurture their children's spirits. But, in a tiger-parented household, it's the opposite—and until the tiger-parented cub is able to cut ties from their parents' identities so that their identity is their own and they can be happy and fulfilled in

---

2. "Codependency," *Mental Health America*, https://www.mhanational.org/co-dependency#:~:text=It%20is%20also%20known%20as,relationships%20in%20families%20of%20alcoholics.

that identity, the trait of codependency will continue to linger, until it is cut through deprogramming.

A lot of this codependency plays out in the form of our Asian American parents' generosity: a mix of criticism, disapproval, and "acceptance." And this generosity supposedly doesn't have strings attached—but we all know that it does. Why? Because it's all about control. (And, of course, codependency is all about control.)

It's fair to say that I've been codependent with my parents throughout my entire life. And while I've made great strides over the years (which we'll get into later), I still to this day sometimes notice their hold on me in one form or another. I had tried dozens of times to cut that cord, and yet I still had a hard time saying no to my mom's help. I struggled to draw a boundary and say, "Hey, Mom, this is my life. I am accountable for my choices and how I react to you." I worked with many therapists and energy workers, and each treatment always started with reconciling my past. I attempted to break down the past, embrace life in the present, accept my mistakes, and move on. It's like the old American saying, "The only way through it is by being in it." But, for a long time, I couldn't break those bad "tiger cub" habits. I wanted to insert my own voice and my own will, to live the way I wanted to live and be who I wanted to be, but I was met with defeat each time I would cave instantly when it came to family pressure, and I continued to work according to my parents' rules.

I had learned early that it was a futile exercise to try to defy the controlling thumb of the tiger mom. Before I had learned this hard lesson, I had been especially defiant—and my mother would wash my mouth with a bar of soap. My mom liked the Ivory brand because she thought it was clean and pure, with the smell of coconut combined with the freshness of a babbling brook in a mossy, overgrown forest. At one time, I got my mouth washed at least once a week for a stretch of three or four months. During that time, I liked to let my mother know that I didn't agree with her opinions, or that I thought her opinions were just wrong; which, as she showed me each time, was something a tiger cub should never say to their Asian mother. It would start with just a conversation, not an argument, but it always ended with me thinking that I had been doing something right because my mother had told me one thing but then wanted me to do something else. Even when I thought I was adhering to her rules, the rules would change, and I wasn't told that they'd changed. In many of those cases, those conversations ended with her saying, "Victoria, I just don't know what to do with you. I'm going to have to teach you." And then I'd inevitably be dragged down the hall to the bathroom to get my mouth washed out. By the end of those three or four months, I would just grab the soap and hand it to her when I knew I was in trouble. It was only after several more occasions like that when I finally learned not to say anything. Although flawed, this was my mother's method to simultaneously demonstrate love and control.

My mom, as all good Asian parents do, wanted to ensure that I had the best of everything. That's what washing out my mouth was about, so that I could learn and listen and understand the boundaries around me, so that I could have the best of everything. To have the best of everything, my mom had to oversee or correct everything I did, so that I could be perfect and meet or exceed the expectations that had been set in front of me. For example, my mother did my homework all the way through high school so that I would get good grades and get into a good college. Incidentally, I found out only in college how to do homework and get graded on the work that I did. This control and codependency lasted through high school and through my adult years as I continued to color within the lines of who I was expected to be and what I was expected to think. It was like being in a prison where I was not allowed to find my voice and experience all that life had to offer.

While I was growing up, my mother used crying as a way to exert control through shame and guilt. She would cry about finances, how poor we were, and how sad she was that we were a disappointment to her because we were not doing something right, because my dad did something she didn't like, and so on.

My sister and I would often say to each other, "Where's Mom?"

To which the other would reply, "Oh, she's crying again."

"About what this time?"

And invariably, it would be about something we wouldn't even bother to remember just a few hours later. That's how often she cried.

Oftentimes, my sister and I would be compelled to listen to her as she bellyached or complained, and we hoped that by listening to her, she'd feel better and would move on. There were many times, however, when I caved and did whatever she wanted, just to make the crying stop. There was always some guilt lurking in those moments, and it was during those high-intensity crying episodes that she coupled manipulation with guilt. Like when she cried about my dad and finances.

"Victoria, you never want to marry somebody like your dad, who is irresponsible about money. I should have married the optometrist. Now I'm left with all these bills."

Whenever she cried about that, I swore up and down that I would never marry a guy like dad. And, from my first date, I cared about the pedigree of the guy and whether my mom would think he met her standard of being responsible with money. As I got older, it would be my mission to never marry someone who was like my dad. I vowed to find someone who could take care of me. I looked for—and found, time and time again—someone who was a doctor, a lawyer, a financial manager, or an entrepreneur who had accomplished something. And I became super diligent about watching my finances.

She also often cried about how we couldn't afford anything.

"Victoria, we're so poor. We can't afford a pretty dress for you right now. We'll have to wait until later." Or, "Victoria, we're so poor. We can't afford much right now, so whatever you were going to ask for, can we wait until later?"

One time, when I was a junior in high school, I tried several times to ask my mom for a check to pay for my Advanced Placement tests. Each time I approached her, she cried about our finances.

I was wracked with guilt for asking for any sort of handout, especially during critical times when my parents were stressed about money. So I took matters into my own hands. On the Monday that the check was due, I went to my English teacher,

Mrs. Miller, and asked if there were any scholarships that I could apply for so that I could take the tests. I felt a bit ashamed to ask for help from anyone other than my family, but I was proud that maybe I had found a solution.

Mrs. Miller looked at me and asked, "Victoria, why do you need money for these tests?"

"My mother said that we were too poor to afford the tests," I replied. "I didn't want to bother her with expenses that we didn't need. If I can't find the money, I'll sit the testing out."

Mrs. Miller sprang to life. "No, Victoria. You are very talented and bright. There's a needs-based scholarship that we use for special and gifted children, just like you. I'll take care of the payment for your two tests. Thank you for asking. I know it was difficult for you to ask."

I felt like this huge burden had left my chest and my shoulders. I took both the AP history and English tests in the following weeks and passed with flying colors.

My mother found out about my ask about a month later when I was in the car with her and my sister.

"Sabrina, how were the AP tests? Did you get your scores back?" she asked my sister.

"Not yet," said Sabrina.

It was in that instant that my mom remembered that I was supposed to have taken the tests, too.

"Victoria, didn't you have AP tests as well?"

"Yes. I got my English and history scores last week. I passed," I said.

"Wait, how did you pay for the tests? I didn't give you a check," my mom asked, confused.

"I got aid. The school paid for my tests."

My mom was driving at the time, and I could tell that she was about to veer off the side of the road.

"What?" she exclaimed. "Aid for what?"

"They have aid for people who can't afford the tests," I said. I was proud of my accomplishment in paying my own way.

"I'm going to write you a check, and you are going to pay the school back. We don't need financial aid," she said loudly.

"But you were crying that we are too poor. So I wanted to help."

"You need to take the check."

"But I'm not going to. It's done." I looked defiantly at her. I knew that I had done something that was actually productive. Just because my mother was embarrassed didn't mean that I was going to give the school the money that I had believed—and that she had claimed—we couldn't afford.

I could tell my mom was appalled at the situation, and she was struggling to figure out what to do next.

Being a tiger mom, she believed that her children's educations should never suffer, under any circumstances. It was at this point, when I was fifteen, that my mom realized that her behavior of ranting on and on about being poor really did have an impact. After that incident, I don't remember her crying about finances—or, if she did, it was done in private.

Another time my mom used crying as a form of control was when I was in my twenties. This was the first time in my young adulthood that I tried to find my own voice, to find my own way and be emotionally independent from my family. My mother hated a boy that I had fallen in love with during college. Four years later, she thought I would have outgrown my love for him—and I hadn't. For this, she cried and tried to convince me to break up with him. She thought he wasn't good enough for me (and many other tiger moms would have agreed). At the time, I was working as a marketing assistant at Oracle in San Francisco; this was not a particularly enviable or important role, so I didn't know why she was being so harsh, but she was afraid that he wouldn't amount to much when he got older.

Drew had been born with a silver spoon in his mouth. At six feet five inches, he should have been a star basketball player, but he wasn't able to pursue that dream due to a bum knee. When we were in college, I helped him with his homework, and he had little to no job prospects after college. Despite this fact, Drew was the love of my life, and like many headstrong college graduates, I decided to say something about it.

"Mom, I'm leaving Oracle to go back to Seattle. I can't stand it here," I said.

"You're going to throw away your career to go back to that loser? Are you trying to shame me in front of the aunties? Do you want to take care of him for the rest of your life like I do with your dad? I can't have you live that life."

"What's wrong with your life with dad?" I asked.

"I have to do everything! I don't want you to marry or be attached to someone like that."

I could tell that my mother wanted me to do well—to marry well—so that I would be financially comfortable, but I didn't listen.

Shockingly, my mother did something I never thought possible: she supported me, and she even helped me move from my old job in California to my new job in Portland, Oregon. I had gotten a job at Waggener Edstrom to be closer to Drew, so he could move in or come down if he wanted to.

My mom's parting words were: "We love you, Vic. If you want to screw up your life with this guy, go right ahead. Just don't let me say I told you so."

I knew my mom wanted me to make it on my own, and she knew that I'd find my way…just as I had when I went to college. Her whole goal in raising me in this tiger-mom parenting style was for me to successfully launch. While she instilled the operating system that I abided by—being driven, resourceful and confident in my ability to succeed in life—she also knew that, because of our culture of pleasing, I would care about what she thought and would ultimately listen to her. The combination of those two opposing factors made me really listen to my mother's words.

And her words ("If you want to screw up your life with this guy, go right ahead"), of course, haunted me. The guilt that I was potentially going to screw up my life by being with Drew niggled at my conscience. I'm sure you've experienced it, too. One day, you wake up to find that it's flooded every pore of your body. You can't wash off the guilt, even with multiple showers, so you have to act, and act fast. That's what happened to me in this instance. I ultimately caved and broke up with Drew in order to release off my shoulders the weight that I was doing something that my family didn't approve of.

I tried to stand up for myself again when I was twenty-five. Sabrina had just gotten married the previous year, and as a result, my mother was pressuring me to get married. During that particular phase in my life, I loved building houses as a side gig. But, as part of the parameters of a house I had bought, I was living with Peter (my boyfriend at the time).

When my mother eventually learned that I was living with Peter, she began her campaign of crying and shaming. She told me that I was going to embarrass the family by living with someone before marriage. Her campaign lasted for about six months. During that time, I kept bringing up to Peter that my parents wanted me to get married, and that we had to do something about it. Eventually, he proposed. The problem was, I didn't want to marry him. I was worried about Peter's anger issues, and I wasn't sure if I could live with him or his anger issues long-term. I knew those red flags were there, but I ignored them to appease my mom.

The first conversation with my mom went something like this:

"Victoria, when are you getting married?" my mom asked.

"Mom, not for a while," I said. "I don't even know if I want to marry Peter."

"You are living in sin with him! You're an embarrassment to the family!"

"What's your point?"

"He can't always suck the tits of the cow for free."

"Mom, that's so crass." I rolled my eyes.

"Well, you are bringing shame on our house."

"Why do you say that?"

"You just are a sinner." She shook her head.

I rolled my eyes again, thinking that the conversation would end. But my mother and I had the same talk day after day, twice a day, and then three times a day.

The first month, she pleaded with me to reconsider.

"Your Uncle Ray is happy to marry Peter and you," she said. (My uncle is one of the most well-known ordained Methodist ministers in the Hawaiian Islands.)

When that didn't work, she became more insistent and added crying to the dialogue. By the third month, I constantly heard her wailing about how I was living in sin. Month by month, the volume of her tears grew. By the sixth month, it wasn't just me who was living in shame. She was, too. The whole family was living with my shame.

And the guilt from that shame got to me. I caved at the six-month point. Peter asked me to marry him, and I said yes—even though, deep down, my heart said no. I chose not to listen to my inner voice at that point because I believed that my needs were less important than my mother's need to eliminate the shame that I had been causing the family. Making the choice to get married was the least I could do to ease her suffering.

So it was the happiest moment of my mom's life and the worst moment of mine. My mother, however, didn't care. She was too worried about appearances, and she told me that, if I didn't marry him soon, I would bring more shame to the family. Throughout my engagement, I wrestled with balancing meeting my family's needs and my own. I expressed my concern to my sister, my cousin, and my mother, but it didn't seem like anyone cared about my needs. Multiple times, I told my mother that I didn't want to go through with it during the engagement; and each time, out came the tears again. Her story was always the same: I was living in sin, and I was an embarrassment to her.

In short, I got married because of the control my mom was able to exert through her tears and the pressure she put on me to preserve my family's reputation. I couldn't live with the shame of being an embarrassment to our family, and so I succumbed to the rules of the tiger mom.

The first time I successfully broke that control and firmly stood my ground was when I was around thirty, when I refused to take money from my mother.

What's terrific about a tiger mom is that if her cub gets into trouble and can't get herself out of a hole, the mom will get involved. And my mother did just that. About two years before I got divorced, Peter and I had been working on a building project—remodeling my house—and we were supposed to be following a budget. Using a tactic that my mother had used (which I learned later in therapy is called gaslighting), Peter questioned my skills, saying things like, "You just don't know what you're doing," or, "It's obvious you don't understand," or, "You are trying to control me," or, "This is not your area of expertise. Why are you trying to insert yourself where you just don't belong?" As a result of Peter trying to control the budget (without being the project manager or the person paying the bills), the construction expenses escalated to a point that was unmanageable. We had not only exceeded the amount that I had budgeted for, but we also took a loan from Peter's parents, used up our credit line, and maxed out all of our credit cards—over $185,000—and we still had more bills that totaled in the high seven figures. The total was over $685,000 for the remodel.

After the remodel was completed, I wanted to refinance the house to get out of the mountain of debt that I—as the sole wage earner—was paying, but Peter refused to sign any paperwork to refinance. He wanted to sell the house in a market where the house wouldn't sell—it was 2003, during an era when houses just weren't selling easily. I pleaded for Peter to work to help pay for some of the costs, but he also refused to work. So my mom stepped in and volunteered to provide me with a loan. She couldn't stand to see me in a mountain of stress and debt. Somehow, I found a way to say a resounding no to my mom.

"No, thank you, Mom."

"But Vic, look at you. You can't continue to do this, paying for everything and pretending that everything is OK when the financial stress is eating at you."

"I'll figure it out, Mom. I always do."

"You'll go bankrupt. You can't have that on your record. It will look bad." My mom was always concerned with what others thought.

"I'll be fine, Mom." I was determined, resolute in figuring my way out of the hole that my husband had created for us.

I could tell my mom didn't like my reaction to her generous offer of bailing me out of debt. My mom was rightly concerned about my finances and how the stress was impacting my life. She saw me repeating her pattern of worrying and being responsible for finances, and she didn't want me to go through the same type of burden that she had gone through, worrying about everything. Turning down her money was the only way that I would be able to land on my feet, without the safety net of my family. And, while it was terrifying, I was intrigued at the prospect that somehow, miraculously, I might have the capability of rebounding out of debt. Besides, if I didn't say no now, when would I ever cut the cord?

The problem was that I was working and was in law school at the time. To pay off the mountain of debt, I put my law school classes on hold and took on additional clients to pay for the cost overruns. I then got creative on how to work my finances. It took me two months to find a way out of the hole. I talked to a variety of people, and I eventually talked to my attorney who provided me with an out to refinance all the debt. Because my husband had refused to sign any paperwork to refinance the home, I got a court order to declare him mentally incompetent so that I could do what was necessary to gain financial stability in this quicksand of debt. After a series of conversations with Peter—during each of which he said no every time—he eventually agreed when he saw the paperwork asking the court for a hearing date to call him mentally unfit to make financial decisions. Several days later, the refinancing was completed and the stress was relieved.

After that incident, I realized that I had the strength and the ability to exercise and use my voice. I could find my own way, outside of my mother's control. Two years later, I cut the cord by divorcing Peter, the man I felt that I had been shamed into marrying. I finally did what was best for me (even though it was only after Uncle Reynold had deemed being divorced as acceptable). At that point, six years of marriage had passed. Six long, miserable years of marriage to a man I didn't love, a man I had married because my mother wanted me to be married. That was the stronghold of my mom's control: guilt and shame.

I already knew what my mom's reaction would be. Divorce—like a mental disorder or a health problem—is not something a tiger parent even acknowledges. It's looked upon with disgust. It's the equivalent of having a red mark on your back—the mark of a divorced woman. I had tried on many occasions to tell my mom that I wanted a divorce, only to be met with negative comments about her divorced friends.

She'd say, "Oh, look at Penny. Her husband left her to raise three kids. I hope the alimony and child support cover her costs."

Or, "Poor Stella. Reynold inherited his family's holdings in real estate. He did really well and doesn't have to work. He divorced her and traded down for Beatrice—a woman twenty years younger. Stella gets nothing."

In most cases, she shook her head in disapproval.

After eight years of being together, including six years of marriage, Peter showed his true colors. Not only was he an abuser, but he had also cheated on me many times. For example, he went for a drink with "friends" the day before my twenty-sixth birthday and came home the next day smelling of perfume. On four occasions, our local dry cleaner took me aside to point out lipstick stains on Peter's shirts, stains that she wasn't able to get off his trousers near the crotch, and stains on the collars of several of his jackets.

While I tried to say that I wanted out, and wanted out badly, it took me a long time to do it because I feared my parents' judgment. Getting a divorce—even though it was a bad marriage—would be a badge of shame; it would mean admitting that I had failed at something that was seemingly important to the rest of society. And I knew it would be worse if I told my mom the circumstances.

Then Peter went to a Tony Robbins-style self-discovery retreat in the backwoods of British Columbia to discover his true purpose. While there, he met up with a woman named Brandy Lawless. (Yes, that's her real name.) At the time, she and Peter were real estate agents working out of the same office. Peter had found the retreat through work.

"It's five days long, and it's supposed to inspire me to find my real desire. By finding my desire, I can triple my sales," Peter explained.

"If it will help your sales and help you find motivation for work, I'm in," I said. "I can go too, right?"

"I'm going with work colleagues. I can expense it."

"Who?" I asked. He listed a few of his colleagues who had signed up, including Brandy, who was working for us to sell one of our properties at the time.

During the retreat, I remember having a phone conversation with Peter, when he called to announce that he was leaving me.

"Vic, I'm leaving you for Brandy," he stated.

"Peter, can you please give me a bit more context?" I asked hopefully.

"I'm not happy. We haven't been happy for some time. I learned this in camp. Brandy makes me happy. She gets me, and she inspires me."

These aren't words that any tiger cub wants to hear. Tiger cubs get it right. We're perfectionists. We're the ones who get picked, not put aside. We never fail.

I imagined the conversation I would have with my mother. Obviously, this wasn't something that would roll off the tongue. I didn't know how to explain this situation to my friends. I definitely didn't know how I was going to explain this to my family. I imagined that I'd say, "Hi, Mom and Dad. I wanted to let you know that Peter and I are getting divorced."

"What's her name?" they'd ask.

"Oh, Brandy. Brandy Lawless."

"Victoria, he traded down for a hooker?" Their shock and disgust would be palpable.

"No, Mom."

"Brandy Lawless is a hooker's name. Do you have to pay him for leaving you?"

"I don't know, Mom," I'd reply.

"He ran away from you, and you may have to pay him. You were the breadwinner. *Aiya!* What do I tell my friends?"

There would be anger in my mother's voice. Not only would I be embarrassing her because I was getting divorced, but I would be embarrassing her because of the way it had happened. I, the golden child—the one who seemingly had everything—was in fact getting thrown over for someone markedly inferior. I was a bit insulted (at least it was insulting to my ego) that Peter had run off with not just a coworker but with the real estate agent for our property, a woman with a name worthy of a woman working at a topless bar. Although I was going through one of the most significant changes in my life, I was more concerned about how my mother would look in front of her friends than I was about my own well-being or what people thought of me.

If you've been parented by a tiger mom, you know exactly what I'm talking about in all of these scenarios. You know what it means to be under the control of a tiger mom; to be a dutiful and respectful cub; to aspire to the dream your mom has for you, regardless of whether it has anything to do with what you actually want. Worse, if you disobey her wishes, you'll have to live with being publicly shamed in front of your own family. And if something like my divorce happens to you, you can imagine the tap-dancing and the backpedaling that would be required to get into favor with your family again, to not have them give you that look of disappointment, to not have that embarrassment and judgment hanging over you.

Like the countless other times when my mother had let me know that I was being difficult because I had said something that she didn't like or wasn't in agreement with, I had gone against her authority and had not done things the "right" way, the Asian way. And, while I was not being intentionally defiant, my mom felt that my actions were inappropriate for how a daughter should behave.

But, in the case of my divorce, my mother was fine with all of it. She was not concerned as much as I thought she would be. I had already thrown Peter out of the house the year before. And now that I was going through with it a year later, my parents—or, more specifically, my mom—supported me in the best way they could, by being available for my calls. When I brought up the hard stuff, like how I felt, my mom deflected the conversation. But the availability of having her listen to me provided me with something of a foundation to start growing while I was grieving for a life that was changing.

It was with this divorce that I began exercising my voice and trying to not be concerned about what my family thought or how I could satisfy their emotional neediness. I realized that my needs mattered, and I was stepping away from my mom's control. I realized that I was an individual, and that it's hard living a life that looks great on the facade but is just miserable as you live it day to day. As I began speaking up for myself, drawing boundaries became easier. And I started teetering on finding my identity: what I stood for and what my spirit was guiding me toward, versus what my parents wanted for me.

When I started exercising my freedom of choice to combat my mom's control, I started having my first real conversations with my mother. You may have had this type of conversation—an open dialogue of sharing. It's where you can talk about your life without really caring what your parents think about it or what judgments they may have about what you are telling them. That's what I mean by real conversations. It was at that point that I not only experienced the choice in the types of conversations that I had, but I also experimented with choices in different types of actions—actions that I never would have embraced had it not been for this newfound freedom: the choice to change careers (changing from a successful PR career to practicing law to going back to my original career); the choice to actually build a house or two on my own; the choice to go to a new-age energy/ communications class in Los Angeles every week for a year and continue to spend part of my time in Los Angeles; the choice to experience dating and to choose people who were kind to me (people whom my mother would never approve of). Even with my experimentation in actions and the embracing of my newfound identity, I still felt compelled to be who my parents wanted me to be—the driver, the overachiever, the one who had to have a perfect life—when I really wanted something different. And I was still not fully happy with myself.

In my forties, I took a year off from talking to my sister, my parents, and my extended family to learn how to be accountable only for my own life and not for those of my parents and sister. In that year off, I found that I was infinitely happier, and that I could be nicer to myself and stop the negative self-talk and patterns that had led to self-destructiveness. I could open myself up to the possibility that I could have anything I wanted and be anything I wanted to be. And I had so much more energy than I'd had before. Previously, the worry and stress of having my mom and sister approve of everything I did had overwhelmed me, and judgment of never being good enough just seemed to gnaw at me, until the only things I could do were veg out in front of the TV or sleep. Instead, during my time away from my family, I had my highest revenue, and I actually started dating a great guy and had a somewhat healthy relationship where he thought I was amazing just for being me, and not for everything that I did. That was a glorious year.

I ended up extending that one year off from my family into almost two years, but things kept tugging at me during that time to come back to the family: a family member would get sick, I'd miss having the "twin talks" with my sister, or I'd see the photographs from all the family gatherings I had missed. I ultimately went back to having a relationship with my family, with the intention of trying to break down the family patterns, look at my shit, and undo the patterns of self-destruction while creating new relationships with my parents, my family, and my sister. This was something that I aspired to do because, if I didn't break the patterns of control that bound me, this new version of me—the me that I saw in my dreams, where I was happy and loving every single moment of my life, where I felt my heart at every moment and could be truly excited about what I was doing and live for every moment—that version of me would eventually disappear, until I wouldn't even recognize glimpses of my spirit.

When you start to break free from that control, how do you balance finding your freedom while staying respectful toward your family? This would prove to be difficult to master, but I knew it would be worth it in the end because I didn't want to end up like some other tiger cubs who did not manage to break free.

For example, a colleague of mine, Tina, told me the story of her nanny, Penny, a first-generation Asian American who lived in San Francisco. While Penny's brothers and sisters had left the city for other pursuits, Penny had decided to stay behind to take care of her mother. Bright and spry, Penny was at the beck and call of her mother. Her husband had divorced her because she'd been too involved with her family. While she'd tried to draw boundaries to save her marriage, she was wracked with guilt whenever she didn't go to her mother. Ultimately, the family guilt won out.

One day, Tina stumbled upon Penny crying at the bottom of the stairwell while speaking to her mother on the phone in a mixture of Mandarin Chinese and English.

Tina overhead a quick snippet, and from what she could understand, Penny said, "Mom, I can't come because I have work. I know that you have your doctor's appointment, but I'll call an Uber for you. I know, Mom. You've said that it's disrespectful, but I can't come... Hello? Hello?"

Thinking that she was alone, Penny hung her head in defeat as tears welled in her eyes.

Tina could tell that Penny felt torn.

Penny spotted Trish lurking in the background. "So you heard that," Penny said.

"Go to your mother," Tina said.

"But the kids…" said Penny.

"I'll take care of them. You take care of your mother," said Tina.

Penny then shared with Tina about the guilt that she felt from not going to help her mother. She said that if she didn't go, she'd hear about it from her mother, her father, and her family, and she would be wracked with anxiety and guilt to help her mom next time.

Penny was fifty-nine years old and was beholden to her mother because she had never broken free from her control. Even though she had become a high-performing financial analyst in the past, because she respected her parents and abided by their demands, she had ultimately succumbed to what her parents wanted her to be—in this case, her mother's caregiver. By that point in her life, the control and codependency had taken an ironclad hold on her.

Another example is my friend Marc, a CFO at a well-known technology company. He has a relationship with his mother where he just goes running whenever she calls—because of the family bond and family guilt. Marc was in Chicago for business one time when his phone rang as he was enjoying the sights. It was ten o'clock on a Sunday morning, and he was set to fly home to California later that night. He was excited because he was going to see a Cubs game at Wrigley Field later that afternoon before his flight. It would be his first—it was the Cubs against the Dodgers—a ticket that he'd bought several months before, knowing that he'd be in Chicago for the game.

"Marc, are you coming to family dinner?" his mom asked when he answered his phone.

"No, Mom, I'm in Chicago. I'll see you later this week," he replied.

"Marc, you promised that you'd be home for Sunday dinner. Nina and Papa are coming," she said, referring to his cousin and her father. "We're already preparing *lumpia*, *ginataan*, and *penetbet*—your favorites."

"Save some for me and give them my love."

And then the swearing and pleading began. "Marc, you better come home. This was planned around you being in town. You are the one who wanted to see Nina and Papa."

The negotiation from Marc (the tiger cub) began with him trying to draw boundaries to the unspoken rule that he needed to show up when his parents called for him. "Mom, I didn't organize this dinner. I told you I was going to be out of town until later tonight."

"I organized this dinner because you said you wanted it. You better be home by six o'clock for dinner, and you better not be late. I'll let the aunties know."

And then he heard the click of the phone as she hung up.

Marc knew that calls would go out through the phone tree of aunties—a gaggle of his mother's fifteen closest relatives and friends who easily had access to another thirty friends—and if he didn't show up at dinner, he'd be judged and criticized for not being a good son. So, as he walked around Chicago that morning, he wrestled internally about what to do. Go to his Cubs game, enjoy himself, and experience the family wrath later? Or head home now to avoid the aftermath of Asian guilt? Of course, he chose the latter option.

He caught an earlier flight to make that Sunday dinner; and he put on a brave face, suppressing his disappointment of not attending the Cubs game and not trying the Pig Candy BLT to see if it was better than his grandmother's chicharrones.

He justified it to himself because the game had been against the Dodgers—not a team that he would have normally seen, even though he was excited about seeing the Cubs. And he reasoned that he could theoretically get chicharrones anywhere. To this date, he still has not gone to a game at Wrigley Field, and it's been ten years.

For Penny, Marc, me, and other tiger cubs out there, the discipline, strictness, and guilt trips pushed us to succeed early in life. This was a form of love from our elders, our community, and our parents. But there are consequences that show up later in life. And when we start to see the effects of that dynamic, we can make changes to find a healthier balance. Respecting our parents doesn't necessarily mean holding ourselves back or being guilted or shamed into doing something for our parents. And it's not our parents' fault for pushing us to succeed and guilting us into doing what they want. In fact, I'm glad that my mother raised me to have drive and vision, because I still at this age have a desire to explore life. But I will no longer accept the harshness, the anxiety, the guilt, and the suppression of not being able to voice my opinion or show my family who I really am. I will no longer live a life where I'm unable to be satisfied no matter what I've accomplished, where I don't give myself permission to breathe. I definitely did not want to look back on my life and regret that I'd spent my days living on pins and needles, dependent on my mother's approval. I was determined to break the patterns—regardless of what that might entail for me. It could go one of two ways for me: I'd either break the family patterns and no longer feel the family guilt for saying no to my parents, or I'd definitely have war wounds from trying.

So how do you still respect your elders without going crazy and having the patterns run your life? Honestly, I'm still learning and figuring it out (and I'm almost fifty). But I've developed a few tricks along the way, which I hope you can benefit from, too.

First, I try to be present when I notice the patterns coming up, which typically happens in scenarios where I can't control the outcome, or when life throws me zingers and I have to try to sort through the rubble. One trick that keeps me present is closing my eyes and breathing in three long, deep breaths. With each breath, I feel the weight of my body on the earth, my feet on the ground, and the support of the earth. I then think of at least three things that I'm grateful for.

Second, I try not to react to the situation presented to me. I take a few minutes (or even a few days) to respond to a family situation, only responding when I no longer feel any emotion. This allows me to find other viewpoints and to critically assess the situation.

Third, I visualize the situation before it happens. For example, if I'm going to my mother's house for dinner, I visualize the conversations that will take place; I feel the emotion of the event, the disappointment from my mother, the expectation of being a certain way—helpful, dutiful, ever so agreeable. I imagine how I'll feel about being there, the outcome, and my gratitude for being there and spending time with my parents. By visualizing the situation, I can frame how the conversation and event will take place, without surprises, and without the disappointments that I would have felt previously.

At the age of forty-five, I was presented with an opportunity to practice these tips and tricks and exercise my newfound independence when I was invited to go on a cruise with my mother and father and our extended family of twelve. My parents had scheduled the cruise for the entire family, in order to unite the collective. I knew that this event would likely create an echo chamber for the animosity my parents held toward our family members, which would put all of us on edge. But I decided to join in on the cruise because I saw it as a chance to test myself in breaking old family patterns—a "social experiment" of sorts.

Just think of it: twelve Asians on a boat. It would be an arsenal of great information with moments that could be celebrated and cherished, old family dynamics to sift through, and patterns to identify and break so that I could continue to create my new life and my new way of being.

At this time in my life, I had learned one of my most successful therapeutic techniques while working with a man named Karl Wolfe, a renowned pioneer of a type of therapy called Quantum Cybernetics Movement Feedback. It is an interdisciplinary fusion of technological breakthroughs in video and proprietary movement diagnostics that results in the creation of a new paradigm in the science of communication.

In other words, it's a new-age type of therapy that wraps twenty years of therapy into an intensive, nine-month course. The philosophy behind Quantum Cybernetics Movement Feedback is that "how you do one thing is how you do everything." And the world around you is a reflection of you. By seeing (via the video) how you interact with the world and the patterns that you have, by working with the quantum field (and the movement diagnostics), you can find a new way of being. With Karl's help, I saw how the tiger dynamic had played out in my life and in how I interacted in the world. I was able to change how I interacted with others. When it came to interacting with my parents, however, that tiger parenting remained in the background—like the ancient Asian man whipping the ox, telling it to keep on trekking, to never deviate from the course and never act up. The cultural patterning that sat inside my body was way too deep.

At the age of forty-five, I had tried everything that you can think of to break this Asian tiger-parented cub inside of me. In addition to working with Karl, I tried therapies of different flavors, including neurolinguistics, scream therapy, and talk therapy. When therapy didn't help, I worked with energy workers—Rolfers, acupuncturists, craniosacral therapists, movement therapists, crystal healers, energy healers, energy guides, shamans, energy gurus, life coaches, breath coaches… You name it, I tried it. The energy work healed the trauma to a certain degree, but just like keeping up with a health regimen, I had to keep that energy clear by continually working at it. And while I was cleared for a bit, the patterns always came back. It was like that angry dragon became tame and then became angry again, dragging me with it. I couldn't seem to deprogram myself enough to unhook the control that kept bringing me back to that little tiger cub I once was. It's not like you can walk into an office and say to a therapist, "Hey, I need to deprogram myself." You've got to want to do it yourself, and you've got to find the proper guides to take you there.

Just two hours after I found out about the cruise, I saw Guy Armstrong, my chiropractor. My mother had sent a group email to my closest relatives—forty of my aunts, uncles, and cousins—about how the family (my sister and her family, my mother, my father, and myself) were going on a cruise to Alaska to celebrate my mother's seventy-eighth birthday. When this broadcast email went out to the crew—less than a quarter of the 240 immediate family members—announcing a cruise that I didn't know I'd be going on, I didn't know what to do. A wave of anxiety hit me like a brick.

On my way to Guy's office, I thought about my options. I would look like an asshole if I backed out from going as it would appear to be disrespectful to my parents and would seem like ingratitude for an "all-expenses-paid" vacation (remember, nothing is ever free when dealing with a tiger mom). Or I could go on the cruise, and I may not be all that happy to be there. I was caught between a rock and a hard place.

Literally hundreds of questions swelled in an overwhelming wave of panic and cascaded at the same time in a giant wave of terror. What would the aunts say? Would I be yelled at? Would I be shamed or guilted into going? If I went, could I enjoy myself on a ten-day cruise? I was damned if I went and damned if I didn't go. It was a choice that had no freedom in it.

I recounted this to Guy as I lay on the table. While Guy had chiropractic skills, he also cleared my energy and balanced my chakras. I would go to him when I need clearing and grounding. As he reset my body, I could hear the *hmms* and *mmms* as he felt into my energy field. He lay his hands on my heart and cracked my vertebrae, opening my heart center and my ribs.

"Victoria," said Guy, "it's so interesting. While your mind is freaking out and saying no, your body wants to go on this cruise."

"How is that even possible?" I asked. "As you know, I have a tendency to hurt myself when I'm around my family, not in the razor-to-a-wrist kind of way, but I'm accident-prone—very accident-prone." (I'd been known to trip over cats and dogs while on a run, accidently put a finger through a blender, or walk into a wall—especially when around family. In fact, my family used to call me The Hurricane because I would breeze in and out of a place so quickly, creating damage and chaos in my wake. They wouldn't know what hit them.)

"Your body needs to understand the family dynamic and integrate it," Guy said, with the perspective of a wise guru. "Filipino culture tends to be very loud and opinionated. I can see that in you. Also, there's the Chinese culture: very structured, very into staying within the lines, very protective of family values and their way of life. Because you have both in you, you have a conflict going on."

"Opinionated and loud, very vocal about things, but bound by the rules and apologizing for being so loud? Thinking that things have to be a certain way in a certain likeness?" I asked.

"You said it, sister, not me," he said.

If I looked back at everything that I had done, I could see his point.

He continued, "You need to integrate the family dynamic in heart, body, soul, and mind. And your mind has been resisting the family dynamic so much that you are empowering more and more of your Asian traits—the ones that you don't want in your life. The only way to release the trauma with your family and your body is to merge with it and to go on the cruise."

And Guy added a little plug. "I'm here at your disposal. You can see me whenever you want." (Given that Guy was $425/hour—an out-of-pocket expense for healthcare—I wasn't sure that I'd be able to afford daily or weekly sessions. If I did, I'd be broke.)

But he did have a point. He was making sense. I had tried working with Modern day shamans, psychedelic therapy, and energy people, and yet I still had those darn Asian tiger-parented patterns. And I had spent hundreds of thousands of dollars trying to heal myself with techniques that only lasted for a short while.

I realized that the only way to change this overwhelming sense of anxiety and break free from this Asian tiger parent control was to go through it, to actually go on the cruise. I needed to integrate and merge with the energy. I needed to get complete the work so that the past didn't continue to impact how I lived my life, so that I wouldn't feel guilty about everything or feel shamed by the family.

This would be the only way I would move forward. And if it worked, it would allow me to live my life.

The cruise would be the ultimate balancing act—meeting my mother's expectations while not going crazy. I was curious if it would be possible to be my authentic self within the confines of my mother's rule. I was afraid that I wasn't going to be good enough, that I would fall back into my inclination to try to please my mother by caving to her every whim, and that my habit of apologizing might take over. Would I make a dent and be able to express myself, or would I slide into old patterns?

Leading up to the family cruise, I had been learning to express my emotions as a way to balance discovering my freedom while still respecting my family. This did not come naturally to me—and I know many other tiger cubs can relate. Many Asian Americans might appear to be standoffish. They smile without the smile genuinely lighting their eyes. They laugh only when cued. They hold back their anger, disgust, and other emotions, tending to agree with whomever is the authority in the room. This is a sign of being tiger-parented, of being told that you must unwittingly agree with the emotion and tenor of the room. And any emotions that bubble underneath must be dealt with at another time, in private. Think about it: When was the last time you saw an Asian

American openly expressing suffering and crying over the loss of a loved one? When was the last time you saw an Asian American speak passionately about something?

Why do I bring this up? As a tiger-parented cub, showing any type of emotion is the death knell of the actions that may befall you—primarily anger, punishment, or shame. If we didn't show the appropriate emotion to what the situation, there was always some sort of punishment or tongue-lashing. For example, my cousin Leena inadvertently laughed instead of showing no emotion when her brother, Parker, got punished for his prank of switching out the ketchup in the ketchup bottle with hot sauce. Not only was Parker punished, but Leena was punished as well, because she "appeared" to have been in cahoots with my cousin on the prank. Because of reactions like the one I mentioned above, we learned that if we showed emotion, we never knew who would come up to tell us that that was wrong. We learned that, in fact, our emotions had to be tailored to whomever and whatever was in charge that day—whether we were in a particularly stressful scenario that we were supposed to overcome, or if we could relax and enjoy the day (with many opportunities to positively reframe the day).

One of the earliest moments when I learned this lesson was when I was six years old and had to go to music lessons at the Claremont Conservatory of Music. I remember throwing tantrums before going to my music lessons, wanting to be anywhere other than at the piano. And my mother would sit on my hands until I played, keeping me at the piano for what seemed like hours. She'd drag me to the lessons as I cried and pleaded not to go. But then she'd kick me out of the white station wagon, and I'd dry my eyes off, march into the teacher's room, and smile—holding my emotions until my lesson was over and I could leave the room.

Other times, when I spent time with my aunties or uncles during family gatherings—especially if they wanted me to play the piano when I was really young, or the viola or flute as I got older—if I showed any type of emotion or said anything to contrast what my mother wanted me to say or do, I'd get punished with soap and water. Holding in how I really felt became especially heightened during parties with the Filipino side of my family. With the Filipinos, if I expressed my feelings and went outside the box that they put me in, judgment would wrap around me, sticking to me like plastic wrap.

To show emotion or speak your mind is almost seen as offensive in many Asian American families. And this is part of the balancing act that I referenced earlier: learning to express my emotions so that I wouldn't go crazy, while still respecting my family.

The first battle with my mom came up within a few weeks of her booking the cruise. I had been talking with my cousin Lisa, who had recounted her long and sordid tale of traveling fourteen days with her parents while sharing a room with them.

"Be sure to get your own room, or you'll go crazy," Lisa had said. "Wait. You have your own room, right?"

Actually, I had forgotten to ask. I knew that balcony rooms had been booked for my sister and her family, my mom and dad, and me—but I had naturally assumed that I had my own room.

I was wrong.

I asked my mother about this the next day while at tea at the Fairmont. I had just taken a sip of tea and asked, "How many rooms do we have?"

"Sabrina, Darren, and the kids have one; and you, me, and Dad have another," she said.

My teacup fell out of my hands, smashing on the floor. The waiters came out from behind the curtains and quickly cleaned up the mess. As they scurried about underneath, I gave my mom a look. You know the look: when something is horrifically wrong, and you know you are intentionally walking into a natural disaster completely unprepared—without the right clothes, the right gear, or the right provisions.

"Vic, you made a mess. Don't give me that look," she said. Mom gave me her withering glare, that stink eye that makes me quiver in its wake.

"Mom, I need my own room," I pleaded, my voice growing louder with each word.

She sighed and shook her head. "You are embarrassing me. Don't raise your voice, and don't make a scene. This is not what we do in front of others. You are being difficult. Why are you always difficult?" she asked. " Besides, we won't be in the room most of the time."

I took a deep breath and counted to ten. This sound advice had been given to me by my many therapists throughout the years to help me cool down after being confronted with harsh words from my mother.

I didn't say anything at the time, but I resolved to say something at some point. I was worried that my social experiment was off to a rocky start, but I knew I needed to state my feelings clearly. If I gave in and shared a room with my parents, not only would I have to hear my mother's nitpicking, but I would not be able to sleep, thanks to the loud CPAP machine my father used. I needed my own room. What better opportunity to practice breaking free from my tiger mom's control?

Tips for the Tiger Cub

How to Resolve Conflict

Create two columns. In the header of the first column, write "100 Percent Yes" at the top. In the other column, write "Other." Next, write out a list of where you are 100 percent yes on decisions you've made in your life. Spend as much time as you'd like on this list. Include big choices and little choices. For example, it could be as simple as where you live, the clothes you wear, the car you drive, the house you live in, or how you spend your day. If you are not 100 percent yes, put it in the "Other" column. Maybe these are things like attending family dinner? Work? Does the "Other" column outweigh the "100 Percent Yes" column? If so, then it's time to examine those activities. What can be delegated? Where are areas you can say no? What are the emotions behind that?

How to Identify if a Pattern Is in Control or if You Are

Think back to every activity that you do. (For example, picking the kids up from school, having an argument with a colleague or a friend or a loved one, etc.) When you do the activity, are you present? Do you find that you default to the same conversations? The same behaviors? Or do you have enriching conversations each time? Do you have a different reaction to an argument or conversation? When you do the same thing or react the same way when it comes to an argument, the patterns are controlling you.

How to Identify the Impact of Control in Your Life

It's easy to identify where you have control in your life. You just have to look at the things you created in your life and how you do things. For example, look at how you keep your household, how you keep your finances, or how you perform your tasks at work. Is your household neat and tidy? With your finances, did you set up a debit plan to automatically save part of your money in a 401(k)? Those are areas that you can control.

It's more difficult to spot the effects of the controls that you have in your life. Think of simple physics. Each action you take has a reaction.

Write down what areas of control are working in your life. Why are they working? What areas are not working in your life? Is it because you are trying to control it, or are you feeling out of control? These are the areas to pay attention to.

For example, maybe you raise your voice when in a heated conversation with your kids about chores because you are frustrated that the kids haven't done their chores. You are hoping that the outcome of the conversation with your kids will prompt them to do their chores. That raised voice is because of the lack of control of the situation. From the conversation, maybe your kids say no to doing the chores, or maybe they actually do the chores. Regardless of their reaction to the conversation, your kids will have a definite reaction to the conversation. They might always jump when you ask them to do things—regardless of whether you raise your voice. And, while the raised voice may have been effective at getting what you want, your children's reactions to your requests going forward may not exactly be the reaction you want. They may be scared of the next interaction that you will be in, or they might tune you out or react in defiance going forward.

These areas—where you feel out of control—are areas where you can change the outcome of the result. Ask yourself these questions: What would happen if you didn't try to control the situation? Could you do something differently? How? What are the different ways that you could have had the result you wanted? By understanding the impact that you have on others because of your control, you can then choose a different outcome.

How to Balance Freedom from Control with Respecting Family

One of the hardest things about the amount of therapy I've done is realizing that I've given up my freedom all those years to the patterning that I had learned while growing up. I gave it up willingly and freely. The key here is awareness and being present when you are with your family, because the reality is that your parents won't have control if you don't give them any.

Before you go to yet another Sunday-night dinner, ask yourself why you are going. Are you going out of obligation?

Are you going out of respect for your family and the aunties? Or are you going because you genuinely want to go and visit? If you don't want to go, but you'd feel guilty for not going, say no to attending. You are respecting yourself and your family by not attending. And, when you do attend a family dinner, you can experience freedom while respecting your family, because you will be 100 percent present.

HOW TO EXPRESS EMOTIONS AS A FIRST STEP TOWARD FREEDOM
The first step in expressing emotions is to stand by yourself in front of a mirror. Go through the range of emotions in front of the mirror—happiness, sadness, anger, laughter. Really talk out loud and express yourself. How did it feel? What emotions came out? Did you let out only 20 percent of the emotion you were feeling, or was it 100 percent? Do this exercise every day until you start feeling comfortable letting out how you feel to others. It's easier than you think.

Alternatively, sometimes I go into my car and yell. Screaming at the top of my lungs for three to five minutes helps me clear my head and exercise my voice. For me, this exercise is like boxing; I get out all the aggression in a constructive way for my lungs and my throat. This allows me to become 100 percent present and feel confident in how I need to show up in the world. Now, you try it. How do you feel? See if this exercise allows you to feel more confident, more clear, and more present.

CHAPTER 4

Overcoming Criticism

EVERY TIGER CUB IS taught to perform—in front of strangers, aunties and uncles, and pretty much anyone who will listen. It is in our DNA. When we're younger, our parents want to show us off to everyone; not only to showcase our talents, but to show how much they've spent on us and how their money has actually manifested into something that has paid off. And we are, of course, reflections of them, because we are products of them. We want to show off because we want to please our parents and make them proud, and we want to show others how the money and time our parents invested in us has been well worth it. However, the flip side of this is that this pressure that's placed on us inevitably leads to criticism and a deep sense of disappointment when we don't live up to our parents' expectations.

My sister, Sabrina, was always the performer in our family. She always tried to please our mom by performing perfectly at church, in California Youth Symphony, and for our aunties and uncles during family gatherings. She really should have been seen as the perfect child, as far as our tiger mom was concerned. Now, as a grown-up, Sabrina is well-traveled, she's lived on two continents, and she has a high-paying job. She has been married to her loving husband for over twenty years, and they have two bright and precocious kids who attend private schools that cost more than six figures a year. Still, she has saved enough for retirement that she and her husband could retire early. Even with this scenario, our tiger mom wasn't too pleased because, while on the surface Sabrina seemed like a good daughter, the reality was that, on a day-to-day level, her level of performance wasn't high enough according to our mother. There was always something for our mom to criticize, always something wrong with Sabrina or her family. She didn't dress properly. The kids didn't say please and thank you. They didn't respect our mom's views of the presidency. They argued with authority. Her house wasn't big enough… And the list went on.

Like my sister, I was a performer—a really good performer; better than most—but I was anything but perfect. No matter how amazing my performance was, or how proud I might have felt because I had performed well, they always led to disappointment and criticism from my mother and an apology by me.

When I was nine or ten, I played the viola while I was studying at the Claremont Conservatory of Music in Belmont, California. Apparently, I was very good at what I did—so good that my teacher called me a "budding virtuoso with a lot of talent." She had submitted one of my tapes for a national competition, and I was invited to perform a duet with the best viola student in the country—a teenager named Victor. We practiced for weeks and weeks before the competition, perfecting each note. As a younger kid, I was excited to perform with a teenager, and especially the best of the best. When the fateful day came, I was nervous and wanted to perform well. Melodious notes came from our instruments as we stood on stage in front of four judges, each note harmonizing with each other from our memorized pages. Yes, there were a few moments of incongruence, but no slurring of verses, no clashing of notes, and no non-syncopation. After we finished, I knew that it had been a good performance; not our best, but a very good performance, and better than most.

As I walked off the stage, my mother stood in front of me with her arms crossed. Instead of what I wanted to hear, such as, "Victoria, good job. You did well!" I heard just the opposite.

"It was a good performance. You missed the A, the C, and there were times that you were a little flat, but you did OK."

These comments were crushing to me. I felt like my heart had been ripped into a thousand pieces. I had prepared for weeks, only to get an "OK" from my mother. It wasn't exactly what I had wanted. I'd wanted my mother to be extremely proud of me. As a result, I unconsciously apologized, knowing that I would never be good enough.

"I'm sorry, Mom." I uttered.

She shrugged and turned away.

As the judges announced the winners, our names were not called as first place. In fact, Victor and I came in second.

Another couple had performed a Hindemith duet that was perfection to the ears and had received the coveted first place. Based on my mother's feedback, I thought that we wouldn't have placed at all, but receiving the second-place award was OK.

I remember looking up at her; I was just a ten-year-old who wanted her mother's approval.

She shook her head and said, "Victoria, if you hadn't messed up those notes, you would have gotten first place. Remember that for next time."

After that comment, she let my multitude of family know that I hadn't done that well. I'd come in second, but it was OK.

A dull thud went through my heart upon hearing my mom's assessment and her subsequent game of telephone to the aunties. I knew then that I had neglected to put on the protective shell that I called my "armor." When I wore my armor, I didn't show emotion; I didn't let anything hurt me. I remembered to do that going forward; and once I put it on, I never took it off. For me, it was a safe place.

To this day, I sometimes still internalize my tiger mom's critical voice, hearing her disappointment as she said things like, "Victoria, you didn't do this right," or, "Victoria, you did this wrong." And, for many years, no matter how well I did, I continued to perpetuate that self-disappointment. I was disappointed with my choice of profession or my exploration of what could be my profession. Even though I had built and sold a successful agency, rebuilt more than eight houses, and was even a practicing attorney at one point, I was disappointed in myself because I believed I was a disappointment to my parents—even though the rest of the world would have considered me successful. It is the tiger parent's dream to have one of their children become a doctor, an accountant, or someone in finance—that is the ultimate marker of success. I was a communications professional, a former practicing lawyer…and divorced, to boot.

I earnestly tried to meet my parents expectations during my teens and twenties. Growing up, all I wanted was to be a sports medicine doctor. I had been in sports throughout school, participating in both cross-country and track and field. For me, it was a win-win: sports medicine would offer me camaraderie, an active lifestyle, and the ability to help others become their best athletic selves. I saw myself running after football players on the green and treating the jocks, helping them rehabilitate and overcome the injuries that plagued them. I was super excited, and I took all science classes in my first semester in college. However, I quickly learned that I was pretty terrible at the sciences. The D I received in nutrition and the C+ in oceanography became clues to me. I wasn't going to be a pro at the sciences. I had to rethink med school. I should have known this after getting a C- in chemistry for the second time in summer school, but it didn't dawn on me until I got my first-semester grades: a report card of all Cs and one D, with the exception of an A in my communications class.

At first, my tiger-cub self kicked in with the self-inflicted hatred and disappointment that I had learned growing up. My inner voice spoke to me. It said, *Wow, that's bad. Victoria, your parents are going to kill you.* (And that voice sounded eerily similar to my mom's criticisms.)

And then another voice—an intuitive, knowing voice—started joining in. "OK, Victoria. Go where you have As." So I set myself up to be a voracious learner in a double major in communications and English. Those subjects were just natural fits. Once that image of me chasing down athletes had faded, I saw myself as the next Connie Chung. Truth be told, I had always seen myself as a better Connie Chung. I had been excited that an Asian woman had broken the mold to be a rock-star interviewer on TV, but her lack of expression and the terrible questions she asked her guests always stunned me. I thought, *Why is she asking that?* Or, *Did she actually ask that?* Or, *Why is she not relating to her guest?* It was like she never read body language when interviewing her guests, and the network just wanted to have her as their token Asian.

So I was super excited when my communications professor, Ray Preene, recommended me for a six-week summer scholarship in Atlanta, Georgia, to learn about television journalism. I called my mother, expecting her to be proud of me for being recommended and for doing something different than my planned summer job in marketing at Oracle.

"Mom, guess what? I'm going to pursue my dream to be a television anchor. I'm going to Atlanta, all expenses paid, to learn about television journalism. I'll be the next Connie Chung."

The sound of the phone dropping to the floor greeted my ear—not the enthusiasm I had wanted to hear. When my mom finally picked up the phone, I heard what sounded like an owl screeching at the top of its lungs.

"You *what?* After a year of college, you want to go into television journalism? You'll make no money as a television journalist. How are you going to support yourself? What are you thinking? I'm not going to support you for the rest of your life." Then she mockingly laughed. "Eddie, did you hear that? Victoria wants to be a television journalist."

I had seemingly caught my mom when she was having coffee with my aunts, and it was going to be a source of conversation now.

I could hear Auntie Eddie—who was not a tiger mom—in the background, arguing with my mother. "Lyn, what's wrong with television journalism? She needs to explore what she wants to be."

(Go, Auntie Eddie. It was a rarity that my aunts stuck up for me, and I appreciated it.)

"She's not going to make any money if she pursues television journalism. It's not going to happen," my mom said to her.

She spoke into the phone. "OK, Victoria. It's your decision. Do what you need to do. But I'm not going to support you if you go this route. I need to finish my coffee with my sisters. I'm saying goodbye now." And I heard a click.

So I was left with a choice. I could disappoint my mother forever if I explored what this scholarship might lead to, and I'd be doing what I really wanted to do. Or I could follow the path of what my parents wanted me to be and work in a profession other than all the choices I'd given them thus far. In their eyes, if I was an accountant, technologist, doctor, judge, or someone in finance, I was in a favorable field. The criticism, disappointment, and disapproval were fierce in my family.

Imagine a feeling of guilt, like your heart is being pulled out of your body in a way that you can never repair. You want to make up for it, but that heartache is so fierce and everlasting. That Asian disappointment and guilt ultimately led to my direction in life. I gave up on following my heart, and I decided to do what my parents wanted and what was expected of me. Just like what's probably expected of you. Most tiger cubs have had to face this kind of choice at one time or another. In fact, my Asian friends and I joke that our lives are not our own; they are our parents' lives. We laugh that our chosen professions (a dancer, a violinist, an actor) would have never satisfied our parents' quests for us to have white-collar jobs.

Ultimately, I barely held it together through an early college graduation. (I graduated in three years with two majors.) And I have since been a disappointment to my mother, even though I followed the path she wanted me to follow. And I have my other pain points—some of which I had kept secret—that have reinforced my disappointments and reminded me of my constant failures. Some of these I haven't yet shared with the world; but I'm sharing them with you now, in the hope that it will release the shame and guilt: I suffered from bulimia when I was younger; I almost ran away on the day of my wedding with four hundred guests; I had a failed marriage and a failed first business venture (my business partner died, and I sold the business); I chose to become a lawyer, and then decided to quit that profession; I managed a short sale on one of my properties; and, at the ripe age of forty-eight, I currently don't have kids or a husband. I didn't look at what the world saw: a successful business owner who owns multiple properties around the nation; a well-published voice in my field; a well-known pillar in my community; a fully funded retirement; and experiences traveling to over twenty countries. Instead, all I heard was that critical voice of my mother, because in her eyes—and in my eyes—the list of failures was the only thing that stood out.

Similarly, this dynamic of criticism found its place within my relations with my cousin Kate. Our cousin moments were few and far between. They were always moments of drama that showcased the reality of our upbringing and our uncertainty of where exactly we stood with each other and in the family. Kate encapsulated all the elements of our Asian upbringing: the self-deprecation, the guilt, the criticism, and the ability to take what could be an amazing experience and turn it into drama. It ultimately robbed her of joy. All of this was a by-product of the pressures that had been placed upon both of us.

In my mid-thirties, I took a trip with Kate on a ten-day adventure to Italy and Croatia via plane, train, and automobile. We saw the most pristine beaches in Croatia; and we visited Dubrovnik, Split, and some of the islands. We saw the Amalfi Coast and tasted wines in the mountains of Italy. We stayed in castles and on farms (agritourism) in the Tuscan region, eating and drinking our way through the countryside. In each picture that she took, we were smiling, looking like we were having the time of our lives. However, my memories of the trip are of her yelling at me and being mad at me in each city while I navigated her moods.

Kate often complained that things were "too expensive," laying her judgment on nearly every expense. Once, Kate wanted to go to a place in Tuscany for *bistecca alla*

Florentina—a famous Tuscan delicacy. We found one of the most highly regarded places in Florence, on a narrow street overlooking the river. It was a tiny, cozy restaurant with only fifteen tables. The staff spoke little English, and they served food family-style. We ordered half of the steak order to split between the two of us, as we thought it would be a huge order. Dish after dish came out—in total, almost eight dishes. The wine came out, and it was free-flowing. Kate went into hysterics about the bill after the fourth dish came out—and this was before the steak and the dessert.

"Victoria, that's going to be too much. We accidentally ordered the wrong meal. They didn't understand us."

"Kate, don't worry about it. The bill's on me. Just enjoy it."

"We can't afford this meal," she countered.

It was that Asian guilt of enjoying something rich. But I reiterated, "I got it."

It was obvious, however, that Kate didn't believe me. As she sat there panicking, a juicy, red, raw piece of meat came out on a large platter the size of a serving tray. The meat overflowed the seams of the plate as the waiter tried to gingerly put it down so that the meat wouldn't touch the table.

I ate what I could—maybe six to seven ounces, max. It was, after all, a raw cow. Surprisingly, Kate tried to eat the entire thing so that there weren't any leftovers. As I sat back in my chair in the dimly lit restaurant, I marveled as she stuffed her mouth full of raw steak.

"You don't have to eat the whole thing. We can take it back to the hotel," I pointed out.

"We paid for this. We need to eat it," she said between bites.

I just continued to watch her, fascinated. It was almost like she wasn't chewing; she was just trying to swallow as much as she could. It was a sight. I was amazed at how her stomach had the capacity to hold that much meat, given what she had eaten prior to the actual steak. A couple of times, she even adjusted her pants, reminding me of an eating contest that I'd seen on TV. How could that be enjoyable? Here we were in these beautiful surroundings, and it seemed she was consumed by the judgment and criticism she had placed on the expense of the meal, to the point where all she cared about was that she eked out each precious dollar being spent. This was where Kate and I differed. For me, experiencing good food in a foreign country was all about the experience, not about the price tag. I saw how the tiger-parented judgment influenced her to hate the fine dining experience that we were having.

When Kate was done, only a small piece was left on the plate. She was proud that she had eaten as much as she could. From my observation, it must have been eighteen ounces of steak. The waiter cleared our plates and then brought out a tiramisu and an aperitif, which happened to be a regional port of some sort.

"Sir, we didn't order this," Kate said to him, frantically tapping his arm.

The waiter smiled warmly and said in broken English, "On the house."

I sat there watching the exchange, wholeheartedly enjoying it, knowing how uncomfortable my cousin was at being "watered and fed" when she was uncertain about the bill.

Then, at the end of the meal, the bill came, and I paid for it.

"Kate," I said, "I'm sorry that you were so upset. But the bill is only 48 euros."

She looked at me, surprised. "But we got so much food…"

The bill turned out to be the equivalent of 64 dollars, not the 120 dollars or more that Kate had been expecting. If she could have just let go of those critical thoughts about the price, she could have enjoyed herself—and she would have been pleasantly surprised by the total bill in the end, anyway.

I grabbed the bill and gave the waiter 85 euros—a hefty tip for such an enjoyable meal.

"Don't worry about the bill," I said with a smile. It was one of those smiles you paste on when you know that it's necessary, but you can't seem to muster the joy to meet that smile, knowing that the other person is sitting in their discomfort. I wanted to take away her discomfort, even though I knew she had been in the wrong.

Later, I faced Kate's tiger-cub criticism once again while on the family cruise. I crossed paths with my Kate, her husband Tom, and her stepdaughter Ann near my room.

"Hi, guys," I called out as I walked toward them, my roller bag and backpack in tow.

I was prepared to give them hugs, but Kate gave me a look. (You know, that look of death that you get from your mother or a relative when they're not pleased with you.) I hadn't seen her or spent time with her since our trip. She didn't have much love for me at that point, as she thought I had been disrespectful to my mother and father when I had stayed away from them for that year. Plus, during that time, my mom and dad had managed to tell the family about every one of my wrongdoings over the last ten years, including that I didn't spend much time with my parents (which was appalling in the family's eyes, given our level of "closeness").

"You're here. I'm surprised that you actually came," she said as she looked me up and down.

Her Debbie Downer attitude was so extreme that it gave me a sinking feeling in my gut. My smile drifted away.

"Why would you say that?" I asked.

"I'm appalled. The way that you treat your mother is trash. I paid a lot of money for this trip. Are you going to ruin it for the rest of us?" Answering her own question, she continued, "You'd better not. However, knowing you, you probably will."

She took Ann by the hand and stormed off.

"Hi, Auntie Victoria," Ann said, smiling at me as she was dragged down the hallway.

"Um, hi, Kate. It's been a pleasure. Really appreciate the feedback here," I said to their backs.

Tom profusely apologized for Kate. "I'm so sorry. She really is glad to see you."

"Is she? It's been three or four months since I've seen her, and I can't believe what just came out of her mouth."

"How so?" Tom asked.

"Well, it's what a tiger mom would have said to get her cub in check, to ensure that she doesn't do something ungracious again. I can't believe she learned that," I added quietly, hoping that Tom wouldn't hear.

"Well, I'm sorry all the same," Tom repeated. He gave me a hug and then hurried after his wife and child. I could see that he was going to try to show her the voice of reason.

"Well, I'm sorry," I said as he left.

Oh, shit! There, I said it again. The apology—the automatic response that I naturally gave when in the face of my mom's criticism. But why exactly was I apologizing to Tom? To Kate's back? I was the one who had been wronged. I had been shamed for just being there.

Shame commands us to apologize for being alive, for just being. But, as we've discussed earlier, there is a huge difference between those automatic apologies that are unwarranted, and the heartfelt apologies when you've done something wrong and have caused another person pain.

For instance, I once almost suffocated my sister at the grocery store. I was five or six years old, and I was curious what would happen if you put a plastic bag over a person's head. We were at Trader Joe's, going down the pasta aisle that was next to the wine aisle. Our mom had just picked up a whole bunch of fruits and vegetables, and there were extra plastic bags in the cart. I was in the main part of the cart while Sabrina sat in the seat. I picked up the bag and read the line, "Bag might cause suffocation." I opened the bag, put it over my sister's head, and held it there (not tightly, but it was still held there).

I stood there, holding the bag while my sister turned different colors—pink, then red, then blue. I was fascinated. At that point, another shopper saw my sister with the bag over her head and me standing there holding it. She alerted my mom, who rushed to us, pushing me aside from my experiment.

"Sabrina!" Mom exclaimed. She was shocked. "Victoria, what are you doing? Apologize to your sister, now!"

It was at that point that I knew I'd done something I shouldn't have, that Sabrina could have been harmed. *Maybe the warning on the bag had been correct*, I thought. However, to be fair, Sabrina had just sat there, and I knew that she had been just as fascinated as I was—even if it would have led to harm. I apologized, and I meant what I said. I didn't want to harm my sister; I was just curious to see what would happen.

That act was something to apologize for. However, aside from sincere apologies, there are those questionable apologies where you are not really sure why exactly you are apologizing; you're just doing it as an automated reaction to someone's criticism (or the expectation of their criticism). Like the apologies I gave to my music teachers for not being the best. When I played a wrong note on the flute, I apologized to Vicki, my flute teacher, that I couldn't carry a tune. When I got a B on a paper, I apologized to my teacher and my mother, saying that I could have done better and promising that I'd perform that much better the next time. When I was late coming home because the bus was late, I apologized to my mother because of my tardiness because the bus hadn't shown up on time. These "flaws" and "mistakes" happened often, and I issued apologies like I was passing out gum.

And the apologizing started taking on a life of its own. It became this unconscious habit that was ingrained in me, in my DNA—and it wasn't just the childhood incidents that I apologized for. I apologized for everything, even as an adult. When I didn't get Christmas presents from my ex-husband, I assumed it was because I had done something wrong, and so I apologized to him for not being the perfect wife. This then made him continually see it as his right to receive apologies from me. Also, when I initially wanted to get a divorce, I apologized for kicking my husband out the door, even though he had cheated on me and was abusive. And in my professional life, when we sold one of the companies for their contracts rather than for an actual company value (because my partner had died), I apologized to my partner's family that I couldn't get more and that I didn't want to continue to run the company. These apologies never served me. In fact, looking back now, I really regret the impulsiveness of these apologies because it essentially meant that I was apologizing for being me.

Similarly, the apology I gave to my cousin on the cruise wasn't an apology I had wanted to give. Sabrina and I had prepared for months to be on the cruise and to face and overcome the negative patterns that we had experienced growing up. But the one thing I had forgotten about was my cousin. When stressed or unhappy, Kate could be your fiercest enemy, like a bear that will tear you to shreds with the force of her roar. I felt like she had shamed me into apologizing just for being there, for standing in her presence. The sheer act of shaming commands presence; it commands control of the situation, until the other person gasps for breath because the air has been sucked out of them. And this one incident was indicative of the family collective that I had grown up in, where fear, shame, and guilt ran me because I wasn't "perfect" like my family expected me to be. If this was how the first ten minutes of the cruise had gone, what would the next ten days be like? I hoped I would not come to regret this "social experiment" of mine…

Tears welled up in my eyes after Kate and her family had left. I didn't want to cry—especially given the recent progress I had made in pulling away from the grip my family once had on me—but somehow, I was so upset by Kate's harsh words that my body betrayed me and showed the hurt that I was feeling.

As I replayed in my mind the scene that had just happened, I realized that the exchange with Kate had given me an opportunity to practice identifying the tiger-cub dynamic in my family. And I recommitted to my intention to break down those patterns over the course of the cruise.

Tips for the Tiger Cub

Tips for Overcoming Self-Criticism

While most self-help gurus will tell you to be kind to yourself and do nice things for yourself, the reality is that just doing things for yourself won't move the needle in overcoming that self-critical "tiger mom" voice in your head. Instead, I find that going to a mirror and criticizing myself helps me get over the sting of criticism from my mother, colleagues, or friends. I'll stare in the mirror and talk to myself really loudly with all the voices I hear in my head. "Victoria, you could do better." "You aren't good enough." "Victoria, anyone can do X, Y, Z better than you." I say as many critical thoughts as I can think of, and I say them in my loudest voice while looking at myself in the mirror. I do this until I can't stand myself anymore; and, for some reason, it changes the energy of those words. The voices calm down. Somehow, something just clicks, and *boom*, that critical voice is gone. Poof. Just like that. I then replace it with the phrase, "Victoria, you are enough." Just the words "you are enough" connote that I have value. My words mean something. My presence means something. And just that little bit of presence means that I matter to the world. What I think matters. Who I am matters.

TIPS FOR OVER-APOLOGIZING

To determine if you over-apologize, keep a log for a week and mark how many apologies you make per day. Which apologies were legit, where you really screwed up? And which apologies were given because you felt like you were expected to apologize? If the number is pretty big—say, more than ten times in the first half of the day—then chances are you have been over-apologizing. To stop yourself from this habit, wear a rubber band on your wrist. Snap the band whenever you find yourself apologizing. Do it lightly, just as a reminder to snap yourself out of the apology and recognize it for what it is. Also, the marks on your wrist from wearing the band will also remind you that you've been overdoing the apologizing.

CHAPTER 5

Releasing Perfectionism

I HAVE A DR. SEUSS painting in my living room, which I got when I was getting divorced in my early thirties. I've kept it all these years because it is representative of how I had been living my life—and how far I've come since then. The painting, called *Fooling Nobody*, depicts a bird, Ted, holding on his head what appears to be a dog. The dog is the persona that people see and interact with. This dog is what people think they are dealing with while the bird, Ted, is doing his own thing beneath what people expect of him and what he shows to the world. According to Dr. Seuss, Ted seems to suggest that no matter how exaggerated, inflated, or different the image we try to portray, in the end what is most important is being ourselves. Because, despite our heroic efforts, we are really fooling nobody when we pretend to be someone that we're not.

This painting represents a time in my life when I would people-please. I'd show people what they wanted to see, I'd be the way that people wanted me to be, and I would reiterate the reflection of the "perfect" woman with the perfect marriage (and then the perfect single life). My life was being run by my perfectionism. The painting serves as a reminder of who I don't want to be—that shadow of the person I once was.

According to Brené Brown, "Perfectionism is a self-destructive and addictive belief system that fuels this primary thought: If I look perfect, and do everything perfectly, I can avoid or minimize the painful feelings of shame, judgment, and blame."[3] We all strive for that "perfection" at times—where we will be free from criticism and judgment—and yet, at the end of the day, that's never the case. According to Brown, perfectionism actually sets us up to feel shame, judgment, and blame, which then leads to more shame, judgment, and blame: *It's my fault. I'm feeling this way because I'm not good enough.* It's not a way to avoid shame.

In fact, in our quest for perfection, we create a life where we're never happy because we're always striving for what others expect of us (or what we think they expect of us). The part of us that experiences true joy gets locked away, tucked under a veneer of other people's expectations. And that authentic piece of us that is truly unique to us gets shoved in a corner—muffled, with its mouth secured with duct tape—until we forget about it; or, just the opposite, until we get to the point where it grows and grows and bursts out to greet the world in an unhealthy way (you know what I'm talking about: bad-mouthing our parents, or getting angry

---

3. Brené Brown, *The Gifts of Imperfection* (Hazelden, 2010).

when we can't control that part of ourselves). That's the impact of perfectionism. It eats at your soul and is often the path to depression, anxiety, and life paralysis.

Perfectionism feeds off of criticism. And, especially for us Asian tiger cubs, it's the by-product of how our parents showed us love. It's ingrained in you as a result of your tiger mom's critical tongue. And her criticism typically takes on a life of its own. As a young child parented by a tiger mom, you probably received criticism for everything you did, from the way you ate and how you dressed to what you said to your aunties and how you performed. The impact of that criticism may have caused you to grow up believing in a state of "perfection" that, in actuality, was impossible to achieve. Your ideal of perfection would be whatever state you'd imagine where your mother wouldn't provide any sort of criticism or "advice," where she would say, "You were brilliant; you are enough."

By allowing that perfectionism to run your life throughout your childhood and into adulthood, you don't know how to be "just" OK, because you believe that your actions are never good enough, that you are never good enough; because you are imprisoned by the familial bond of criticism. In fact, if you allow yourself to be OK, your parents will see you as being disloyal because you're not enabling them to regulate you and push you to do better and be better. As a culture, we defer to the collective and give up our individual selves—and the idea of defining ourselves as individuals scares us. So, for us to make it as grown-ups and be "acceptable" in the Asian culture, we need regulators in the form of our parents and other family members.

Perfectionism also breeds anxiety. For example, I have spoken to several Asian musicians who visualize every performance before they step out on the stage. One of my friends, visualizes putting on her dress, doing her makeup, and then walking on stage, looking at the audience, and picking up her violin and playing. In her mind, she hears the notes as if she is playing them, listening to the violins and the cellos come in when they are supposed to, as her hands travel over the fingerboard and her bow slides gracefully over the strings. This is similar to a technique used by many athletes, but with one important difference: My friend has to be completely alone for at least seventy-two hours before a performance; otherwise, she refuses to get on stage. This hasn't boded well for her violist career as her anxiety is so great that she can't seem to get over her nerves, even after going through extensive therapy.

While I don't have the severe anxiety my friend has, I do get anxious from worrying that things won't go as I'd planned. For example, at my wedding, I had to say the "right" things (to my parents, to my potential in-laws, and to our guests) because, if I didn't, I knew my aunts and my mother would never forget—and they'd bring it up for years to come. That is the type of anxiety that has at times caused me to hyperventilate into a paper bag. It is during those times that I envision myself in a pink tub in a cushy bathroom, screaming into a pillow at the top of my lungs. I imagine my parents and my relatives exploding; I imagine all that I don't want in my life blowing up like a balloon, until it pops and thousands of pieces just fall to the ground like confetti. I then take a deep breath, open my eyes, and pretend to be that "perfect" daughter, business owner, neighbor, etc. without the anxiety I had felt moments earlier.

In the months leading up to the family cruise, my perfectionism anxiety was in overdrive as I envisioned messy scenarios where my actions might result in an unhappy mother, father, or cousin. I could already hear my aunts' critical tongue-wagging if I were to be late or miss the boat. In fact, I had so much anxiety before I reached the ship that, when I actually got there, I was fine. In fact, I was more than fine. In my mind, I had built it up to be such a bad experience where every negative scenario I've had with my family in the past—of being humiliated, of being degraded, of feeling guilty—would be intensified for ten days at sea. But when the day finally arrived, all of that anxiety seemed to have disappeared. Maybe it was the therapy and the long conversations with friends, or maybe it was the two Xanax that I'd taken, but my fear just went *poof*. I was present and had my wits about me by the time I reached the dock.

As I walked through security, I saw the Princess cruise ship. White and twenty stories high, it reminded me of Vegas with its glitz, brass, and casino-like atmosphere. And as I walked on the cruise ship, I realized that it was, in fact, a giant, floating, casino—like the worn and well-known Las Vegas go-tos of Caesars Palace or Aria, , not the plush and upscale feel of the Bellagio. It held twenty floors of cabins, casinos, and restaurants. And as I stood on the balcony of the ship and looked back at the security checkpoint, I saw throngs of families jostling to get on board—a sea of gray hairs and retirees, all smiling from ear to ear, excited for their ten days at sea. Surrounded by the glitz and glamour, and the throngs of people, I started feeling claustrophobic. I took a deep breath and meditated as I walked, feeling the ground beneath my feet, noticing the wind at my back, and tuning in to the noises behind, beside, and in front of me—a technique I'd learned from my therapist on how to stay present. I realized that, as long as I kept my vow to myself—to cut the family cord and let go of the perfectionism that was expected of me—I would be cool as a cucumber because I had never been excited to work so much in my life. I had already planned to work four out of the ten days we were on the boat. By concentrating on my work and on what I wanted to do, I would be respecting myself and reminding myself who I was and what I believed in, rather than allowing the circumstances to dictate how I would act and who I was. This ability to straddle work and family would hopefully allow me to balance my freedom from control while respecting my family.

I was going into this experience with the intention of being my perfectly imperfect self and speaking my truth to my family in whatever scenarios might arise over the next ten days. But one of my worst fears quickly arose as I thought of an email I had sent to my mom to lay down the ground rules of the cruise. I had never set ground rules before with my parents. In fact, setting any sort of boundary with a tiger parent is hard.

One of my tiger-parented friends, Lola, set ground rules for how her parents would communicate with her when she went to college, and her parents held a grudge against her for the length of her college career, until she apologized.

The email to my mom read as follows:

> Hi Mom,
> Wanted to let you know that I'm totally excited for the cruise. I also wanted to let you know that I totally expect us to have an amazing time together. For that to happen, I expect us to have positive and constructive conversations. I want happy times with happy memories.
> To ensure that we have those happy memories, I wanted you to know of my expectations:
> - Enough privacy so that I can be positive (i.e., own room and some alone time)
> - Limited nitpicking of Dad, me, and our immediate family
> - Limited guilt-tripping to do activities, criticism, and public criticism (including and in front of immediate and extended family)
> - 1–2 dinners by myself (ex. I have to work on Wednesday night)
>
> Please also note that I will be working M–W of next week, so you may see me only part of the time. I'd also like to know what your expectations are before the cruise, as it relates to meals and activities and togetherness.
> NOTE: What dates are we having the formal dinners?

Thanks again for everything and confirming that I have my own cabin. I look forward to seeing you at 1 p.m. on Saturday.

Love,

Victoria

I was sure she'd shared it with the aunties and immediate family, and she would have included a commentary about how she had been violated by her children and how I had been ungrateful. I contemplated asking my aunts if they had seen my email, and I was ready to brace myself for their criticism. However, I decided against feeling scared of their disapproval. I acknowledged that my email could have seemed harsh, given all the sacrifices that my mom had made for us, but I had spoken truth to the shaming that had gone on in the subtext of planning for the cruise.

Blinking, I realized that I was standing in an empty hallway, inadvertently crying. I really needed to get over myself. If I was going to stand up for myself and stand in my power to go against the tiger-cub mold, I needed to grow some cojones. I had to get a grip before I saw the rest of my family when we met for safety instructions in about an hour. Searching for my room number, I found the correct door and inserted the key.

Inside, the room was pitch-black. I flipped on the lights to find a ten-foot-by-ten-foot room, adequate as an inside stateroom, but reminiscent of the accommodations of a Comfort Inn with its worn comforter and 1980s decor. It would do for ten days. Before I started to unpack my belongings into the shellacked cabinets, I turned on the playlist that my friend Kate had made for me after a conversation we'd had a few months back. The mix was designed to pump me up, with songs from the '90s, like those by Boyz II Men and Eminem. If this didn't help me with visualizing my power, then one of the dozens of meditations that I had collected over the years would help. For this particular day, I listened to a meditation by Christie Marie Sheldon.[4] And after forty-five minutes of prepping and unpacking, I was ready to take on my family.

As I walked up to the main deck in search of my family, I realized that the cruise line was not designed for singles but for the older "cruising" set. As I had suspected when boarding, while there were a ton of families, the average age must have been around sixty-five. At our first gathering (where I saw and greeted my relatives and my parents) to learn the ship protocols and behaviors on one of the main floor lounges, I looked around and was stunned at what I saw: there were no young people in their twenties and thirties, or even those in their forties. Instead, I saw a diverse mix of happy retirees filling the room. They were all different sizes and shapes; some with canes, walkers, and wheelchairs. And they all looked like they were coming for a good time.

Sabrina, Darren, Mattie, Kristi, and I were clearly the youngest ones in the group. Were the families and the younger generations getting their own presentations on safety protocols? Maybe they had a different set of rules? All I knew was that Kate and her family were in a different room, in a

---

4. Mindvalley, "Heart Healing Guided Meditation: Open up to Abundance and Love: Christie Marie Sheldon," https://www.youtube.com/watch?v=Ckrv0QbtIbg&list=PLcTZ8xyOL50H2pvLSeOEb1fADvD1CHyLn&index=5.

different presentation, and I hoped that their group was filled with younger people. If this was the average age of everyone on the ship, it was going to be a very long cruise.

I whispered to my sister, "I wonder how many medics are on the ship?" I knew that if my mother had heard me, she would have cringed.

Sabrina looked back at me. "Victoria, there are twelve hundred people on this cruise. There's maybe two hundred people here. We just got the retirement set. They are not all retirees, OK?" She rolled her eyes.

Shaming is common in Asian families; it's fuel for perfectionism. And it happened fast on the cruise—within the first hour. Like all the tiger moms before her, my sister had learned that behavior, and it wasn't pretty.

The next time I saw my cousin Kate after her initial outburst was at the dinner table. Imagine a completely empty dining room with more than sixty tables of all sizes, each covered with white linen, and with the blue ocean greeting you for a view. That was what eating at 5:00 p.m. was like—no one was around just yet because it was way too early to eat. After the buffet lunch and snack time at three o'clock, most of the guests had no appetite to eat at five, yet everyone was supposed to sit down for a seven-course meal.

As I rolled up at 4:58 p.m., I saw my family—all twelve of them—in the back corner of the empty restaurant. I felt excitement and anger emanating from the table: my mom, dad, Aunt Eddie, and Uncle Ray were glad to be there; Sabrina, Darren, Mattie, and Kristi were tentatively waiting to see what would happen; Kate was angry at the world; and Tom and Ann were unsure of how to navigate Kate's anger. I didn't know what exactly Kate was angry at—I don't think anyone really did—but it greeted me loud and proud.

"Victoria," she said.

"Hi, guys," I said, tentatively smiling as I sat down.

Our Filipino waitstaff gave us our menus; the main course was lobster. I ordered wine for the table—an Italian blend of Barolo and another grape—which cost around eighty-seven dollars. Kate, Sabrina, and I had each brought two to four bottles of wine with us on the trip, but with all of us at the table drinking, one bottle wouldn't be enough—and everybody was drinking on that first night. It was my night to bring the wine.

"Of course," Kate said.

"What?" I asked.

"You just have to show off, don't you?"

I blinked. "You'll appreciate the wine."

The menu itself wasn't all that memorable, but when it came time to order, Ann didn't want to partake because it was too early to eat. "I'm not hungry," she said.

As we consumed course after course, Ann sat there, not eating, and Kate flashed dirty looks at her stepdaughter. When it came time to order dessert, Ann finally spoke up as the waiter moved from person to person down the table. "Can I have mac and cheese?" she asked.

The waiter stood there, writing the order down.

"You can't order mac and cheese," Kate said. "You missed your chance to order food."

The waiter looked up. "Should I order the mac and cheese?" he asked.

"No," said Kate.

"But I'm hungry, Momma," Ann said, her eyes pleading.

Kate and Ann argued for a bit while the waiter went down the table taking everyone's dessert orders. As I watched this kerfuffle, four heads from the next table turned in unison to look at us, agog that we were allowing the discord to continue. The restaurant was now fuller than it had been but was still not quite at full capacity. The other members of my family either looked down at their laps, made chitchat about the weather, or generally tried to ignore Ann›s public shaming.

As I tried to make sense of what was happening, I wondered when exactly it had become OK to publicly shame others in our family. Had it always happened, and I just hadn't noticed it until now? Or had it happened gradually over the years, creeping up on us, until I only noticed it when with my family? All I knew was that my brain was screaming, *Really, guys? Wow. This is backroom behavior that you don't air out publicly, because we care what people think—or, I guess we used to care what people thought.*

I finally spoke up. "Kate, let her order the mac and cheese. Ann, it's OK to order. You haven't eaten anything."

"She can go hungry," Kate said. "She's so picky. She wants everything her way. She needs to learn."

Ann sat there, silently looking down, not whining or panicking, just wanting food.

"Kate, it's OK," I said gently.

At this point, four more tables had joined the table next to us in their staring. And if this was the first night of a ten-day cruise where we had to sit at the same tables the entire time, we would be known as *that* family—you know, the family that is annoying and harsh, the stereotypical Asian family—*that* family.

I searched for reinforcement, yet everyone was looking anywhere but at Kate and me.

Tom finally jumped in, his quiet voice soothing the air. "Ann, you want the mac and cheese?"

"Yes, Daddy. I'm sorry I'm ordering late. I'm really sorry that I wasn't hungry earlier," she said.

And Tom ordered for her.

Kate threw down her napkin. "This wasn't the way that we were raised," she said, leaving in a huff.

I didn't know what Ann had apologized for, but I could see that she was already picking up the symptoms of the tiger cub, essentially apologizing for the essence of who she was.

While Kate was dealing with her own issues, she was incorporating a form of tiger mom into her parenting style. She was replaying the dynamics she'd experienced growing up. Ann, like me, would grow up with her own neuroses, and she would probably continue apologizing for herself and believing that she's never enough.

I wondered, *What if we could stop this behavior and parent differently?* It was not like Kate would be open to it, but retrospectively, I found myself wondering, what if she was? Maybe then Ann wouldn't grow up under that pressure to be perfect. Maybe she would grow up to be different. Maybe she wouldn't have to go through years of therapy like I had.

By virtue of these thoughts, my social experiment suddenly became a bit wider. It was no longer just about me. I wanted to ask the questions and recognize the behaviors, not just for my own benefit but also so that I could help my nieces and nephews avoid suffering the same fate as me. So, after that dinner, I began to keep a diary where I would write down the behaviors my family could be made aware of to help us all break this cycle of tiger parenting.

I also knew I needed to address another variable in the mix: the way my generation had learned to parent. I hadn't accounted for Kate's behavior being part of the dynamics. I had to navigate and implement a strategy for this—but I didn't yet have the tools to do so. The scene with Kate and Ann was tiger parenting gone wrong; it was pure humiliation. Kate must have experienced some form of shaming throughout her life, which she had picked up and was now carrying into her relationship with her stepdaughter.

Like Ann, I had apologized for most of my life for not being "perfect." I can't remember a single day when I didn't apologize for being me. In fact, I practically entered the world apologizing. After thirty-two hours of labor, my twin sister had popped out screaming—a perfectly healthy baby at eight pounds eight ounces, with a thick crown of black hair. Apparently, I had hidden myself deep inside the recesses of Mom's uterus—high up on top of her kidneys and stomach.

Mom said she had intuitively known that I was in there because she had indigestion the entire pregnancy and always had to pee. It didn't seem possible, if there was only one baby, that she'd have pressure on her stomach and her bladder. She argued with the doctor, "I have another one in there."

"You don't have another one in there," said the doctor.

"No, I'm telling you there is one. I can feel the heartbeat. There's definitely another one in there."

I apparently didn't want to come out. I was happy as a clam to stay warm and just hang out by myself in my mother's womb, especially now with all that space.

The doctor called for a second opinion. Four more doctors streamed into the room. Mom had her legs wide apart as all five doctors, each in a white lab coat, leaned forward, as if they could actually see something. My mom's doctor reached inside her and shook his head. He gently felt her stomach and looked around at his barbershop quartet to validate his opinion.

"I'm not sure," he said.

He called in a sixth, seventh, and eighth doctor. For twenty-one minutes, each took a turn prodding my mother. The eighth, a tall man, had the longest arms. He fiddled around until he found my foot. "When a mother says there's something else in there, there's gotta be something in there," he said. "It could have been anything; but she said it's a baby, and in this case, she is right."

Happily floating in my little cocoon of warmth, I hadn't expected to feel a tug on my chubby, short legs. Three fingers wrapped around my ankles with a rapid and insistent tugging, and I was pulled by the legs as he moved me back and forth like he was cleaning off a pair of sunglasses.

By then, I'd apparently lost oxygen and was turning blue. A breech baby, I had my umbilical cord wrapped around my neck and was suffocating. When I finally broke loose from the pocket of fluid and air that had held me for nine months, I was pulled out, limp, at a mere four pounds five ounces. Unlike my sister, who had entered this world screaming, I was silent.

Since I wasn't breathing, my mom's doctor placed me in an incubator. "I don't know how I missed the heartbeat. It must have been the technology." An apology, but not really. How could he, with all of his years of experience, have missed me? "We missed the heartbeat because she was directly behind the first one. How were we to catch that?"

When you go into the hospital thinking that you are going to have one child, and you walk away with two, what exactly do you do? My parents hadn't prepared for a second child. At home, there was only one of everything. One stroller. One crib. One car seat. Everything was for one child, and they were bringing two children home.

I am sure that I apologized for being there. In my blue state, I probably opened my eyes, blinked, tried to focus, and then spoke in my feeble baby language because my lungs hadn't cleared yet. "I'm sorry for being late and causing you to worry!"

I wondered if Ann would have to go through years of what I had gone through. Somehow, Kate had picked up the tiger-mom traits and had added her own special flavor—what I would consider a harsher take, and one that led Ann to be in fear and at the beck and call of her mother to monitor what she should do going forward. Where was the "good job"? Where was the kindness? Where was the goodness in that kind of parenting? I hoped that Ann wouldn't pick up my habit of over-apologizing, but you never know how a kid will turn out.

With Kate gone, the dinner table on that first night of the cruise became more festive and more polite. Ann tried to navigate through her emotions, keeping her eyes focused on her mac and cheese, and avoiding conversation. I could see that she was struggling to put on her armor to keep her emotions in check. It was like navigating the high seas that we were on.

Throughout the cruise, there were a few more bad nights at the dinner table, reminiscent of scenes from a TV show where an Asian family is seated at the dinner table. You know, the one where the angry, stone-cold elders criticize the younger family members for every comment they make, and they force them to eat because they don't think they are eating enough, even if it is a ten-course meal. During these times (when I wanted to be anywhere other than at the table), the elders made backhanded comments to us younger ones while we all tried to navigate the field. As we endured the judgment of the elders and put on our brave faces while others were berated, I wondered why we'd put ourselves in this scenario and agreed to the cruise. And it happened almost every night of the trip.

On one particular night, I realized how epigenetic perfectionism and "Asianism" is. I saw firsthand how it had been handed down from one generation to the next as my mother switched from one persona to another (from anger to criticism to self-doubt to laughter), and I saw how my sister had inherited that behavior and was using it with her kids. My mother would nitpick on my sister with comments like: "Sabrina, you are not eating enough!" and, "Oh! You chose to eat that?" to "Sabrina, I see that tonight's dinner was a casual one." And whenever Sabrina was criticized, she in turn stressed out her kids by picking on them in the same manner.

My cousin also adhered to and listened to my mother's directives of the persona, not just by criticizing but by yelling at Ann and joking at the end after her wine kicked in, while my aunt just sat back and ignored (or pretended to ignore) what she saw. I felt like I had just witnessed the transformation from Dr. Jekyll into Mr. Hyde, and I was confused when the rest of my family pretended not to see the pattern of epigenetics being passed down at the dinner table.

On another night, we witnessed what happens when an individual disrupts the collective voice. It was a scenario that every Asian tries to avoid, not just because it disrupts the dynamic of calm within the group but also because it creates chaos and infighting among the collective. On this particular night, even though we had set a ground rule to never talk politics on the cruise, the topic came up: Trump versus Hillary.

"The country is doing well because of Trump," my mother said, throwing down an imaginary gauntlet. Her comment had to do with Trump supporting the country and creating jobs through the limitation of immigrants.

At this point, the rest of table—all nine of us on this particular night—were ready to stand up and leave. But the stampede out of the dining room never happened because of a showdown at the table.

Aunt Eddie, who rarely speaks up and normally listens to my mother, stood up from the table. "Lyn, Trump has nothing to do with this. The economy is doing well because it's a cyclical thing. If you are going to talk politics, we're going to leave the table."

At this point in the meal—during the second course—Kristi had just eaten all five of her jumbo shrimp, Ann had finished her soup, and I had finished my salad. We were all waiting, fascinated by what my mother would do.

My mother had made her comment while eating her tomato soup, her spoon in the air. When Aunt Eddie spoke up, my mom sat there, blinking, because nobody defies her—the eldest at the table. It's an unwritten rule in the Asian culture that you cannot speak your mind for fear of disrupting the order. Otherwise, your contradictory voice becomes that imperfection in a pearl that otherwise would have been worth five million dollars—if not for that tiny blemish.

The tension was so thick, you could hear a pin drop. The din of everyone else in the dining room seemed to fade into the background. Finally, my mother brought the spoon to her lips and then smiled, the smile that she gives when preparing for battle—a blank look of utter pain. This was going to be a fight for control at the dinner table, a fight for who would own the course of the collective.

The warning shot came. "Eddie, you don't know what you are talking about. But I'll leave it."

This battle could have gone on for a while, but one of us tried to come up with another piece of dinner conversation. My uncle thankfully braved the tide. "Vic, how's business? You are working all the time on this cruise. They don't give you a break?"

"Business is good, uncle. We're in the midst of a transition," I said.

My mother, now on guard, her feathers raised, chimed in. "Vic, you haven't sold the business yet?"

"No, Mom, selling the business is taking a while. It's a process."

I sighed. I didn't know if my mother was trying to make idle conversation or trying to control the conversation—and I didn't like where it was heading, because this was a sore point of mine. I'd had several conversations with prospective buyers, only to have them all fall through. And, at the time, I was in the midst of another hopeful exit that was a costly and time-consuming process.

"How much money will you make, Vic?" my mother asked.

"I don't know, Mom," I said.

"Will you be able to retire?"

"I don't know, Mom."

This banter went on for a while. Thankfully, we were at the end of the main course, and I hoped I'd be let out of explaining everything.

While we were talking, my mother jockeyed for control of the collective, using her tongue to emit both deprecation and appreciation for that which she could control. While she used her wits, I noticed that old guilt creeping in. I felt guilty for not being successful, for not being her ideal of a "perfect" daughter. It was as if my mother was exposing all my shiny warts for the world to see—a public display of humiliation in front of my family. The shame and disappointment overcame me in a bathing of self-loathing, all to show that Mother could maintain control of the collective.

And this self-loathing threatened to stick with me for the remainder of the cruise. However, even though I'd had so many setbacks in selling my business, I knew I had to regain my confidence. And a lot of good things did happen during the cruise—moments when I enjoyed myself and got to celebrate the humanity of being with my family. To help break out of the patterns, my job was to listen and observe behavioral patterns that I wanted to either keep or get rid of without judgment. I spent quality time with my sister, niece, and nephew, creating lasting memories as we hiked up the fjords of Alaska. On these hikes, we didn't nitpick each other; we enjoyed the breathtaking beauty of the greenery around us and caught up on the day-to-day dealings with life and school. I ensured that I had daily morning coffees with my mother and afternoon coffees with my father where I learned about their childhoods and their individual perspectives of life, gathering more insights into how they were raised and getting to know each of them as individuals.

In trusting myself, standing up for myself, listening, and becoming confident in my own voice, it was no longer necessary to suppress the layers of muck from being tiger-parented. And now I had the freedom to get where I wanted to go, to do better and choose better. I was also able to see how my patterns had been running my life. I saw that many of my traits—my self-doubt, my perfectionism, my disappointment in myself, and my need for control—came from my parents and my family. And I was ready to give these traits back to them.

One way I did this was by learning to reframe the criticism I've received from my tiger mom, and the perfectionism it has created within me. As we've discussed, our mothers' criticisms have helped us learn to perform with high aptitude. But, along with this came a downside: we became uncomfortable with being vulnerable because we feared that our imperfections might be revealed. It's a push and pull dynamic where we are unable to show vulnerability for fear of being wrong, being highly criticized, or being ridiculed; but, at the same time, we crave criticism (or attention). The continual stress of this push and pull was—and is—a learned trait of perfectionism that over time has required much reframing for me, so that I could begin to see that I am worthy of self-love, even if I'm not perfect in my actions.

Tips for the Tiger Cub

On a sheet of paper, create three columns. In the first column, write down all the patterns that you see in your life. Do you shop in a certain manner? Do you catch yourself always feeling or acting a certain way about certain subjects like money, parenting, or being with family? In the second column, write down your earliest memory of each pattern. In the third column, write down whether each pattern is serving you now. If it's serving you, write down how it's serving you. If it's not serving you, write down why that is and how you are going to change the pattern. Circle and highlight all the patterns you want to change. Create a series of cards to place around your house with reminders of the patterns you want to change and the new patterns you'll use instead. Over time, with these visual cues, your undesired patterns will dissipate.

CHAPTER 6

Setting Boundaries

I HAD A TAIWANESE FRIEND — let's call him Alan—who, after forty years, mustered up the courage to tell his meddling family that he was tired of being mothered and that he would no longer go on dates that the family wanted him to go on. It was during a Sunday dinner with his family when he decided to announce that he had had enough of trying to please them, that he was tired of their meddling, and that he was happily single. As of this publishing, it has been four years since his parents have meddled—or talked to him at all, for that matter. Because that's what happens when you say, "Hey, parents, here's a boundary." In Alan's case, his parents hated that he had established boundaries. And while Alan was happy that he'd said something, he had not anticipated that his parents would stop speaking to him and inviting him to family functions. In effect, they had cut him out of the family, and this pattern continued until the death of his father.

The Ultimate Self-Help Guide for the Child of an Asian Tiger Mom

Theoretically, we should be able to expect that our family—who have supported us through the thick and thin—would love us and accept us regardless of what might happen. But for Alan—and me, and so many other tiger cubs—it is very difficult to set boundaries because we are afraid that our parents might cut us off from the family in response. In other words, we don't know how to say no. Or "no, thank you." Or the fifty other ways to say that we won't do the thing that we don't want to do.

It was in this vein that, while on the cruise, I was hesitant to tell my family that I had been feeling seasick and wanted off the boat. As a tiger cub, you just don't tell your tiger mom that you are breaking off from the clan. But I was sick. And, wanting out, I braced myself for the largest amount of judgment that I could bear *and* for the shame and guilt of not being the "perfect child" because I couldn't make it through the cruise.

We had just left Ketchikan, Alaska, and were passing the majestic blue fjords on either side when it hit me: the nausea of seasickness. I would have to endure five more days at sea before our return to San Francisco, and I wanted out. As the boat heaved to and fro, headed toward the open sea, I tried to distract myself by focusing on the serenity of being in nature. I tried yet another meditation—this time, it was a Joe Dispenza meditation, along with thinking about deep thoughts by Jack Handy. On this particular occasion, several Jack Handy quotes came to me:

"If you define cowardice as running away at the first sign of danger, screaming and tripping and begging for mercy, then yes, Mr. Brave man, I guess I'm a coward."

And, "If trees could scream, would we be so cavalier about cutting them down?

We might, if they screamed all the time, for no good reason."

Sighing, and realizing that I was stuck on the cruise, I let the beauty of the scenery and the topography consume me. Dark-green forests and ice glaciers surrounded me on either side, with seagulls and other ocean birds flying overhead. I tried to feel my feet, and I imagined putting my toes and feet deep in the dirt in the forest, growing roots.

Then the 800-passenger boat lurched, and the peacefulness that I had conjured for myself turned into dark thoughts. Instead of the green, lush forest filled with graceful deciduous trees, a strange, orangish hue fell like a veil over my eyes. I imagined the contents of my stomach—blueberries, eggs, and coffee—moving up and down with the waves. Could I handle a few more days of being seasick and spending time with my family? Or would it be an endurance test where my body would be in full revolt? (And, if I couldn't handle it, how would I be able to create a boundary and tell my family that I needed to leave?)

My first test, to see if I could stay and complete the social experiment, was to join the 8:00 a.m. cycling class that I had already paid thirty-five dollars for. On that particular day, the class was being given by a perky, blond teacher who, from the looks of it, was a newbie at teaching cycling classes. Super positive and energetic, her cadence was way too high, and her gear was way too low, so that whenever she pedaled, her head moved up and down like a bobblehead doll. And as the boat lurched from side to side, her peppiness contributed to my need to throw up, and the nauseousness made me want to slap her.

I was dizzy trying to follow her lead. All I could see were stars.

"Put your bike on a higher gear on your machine," I yelled stonily.

She looked toward me but ignored me.

I then closed my eyes. At least when I closed my eyes, all I felt were the lurching waves. But apparently she didn't like that.

"High gear! High gear! We're climbing a steep mountain!" she yelled.

Forced to open my eyes to turn the nob to a higher gear, I saw red, and I felt the contents of my stomach rise up in the back of my throat. I should have just gotten off my bike at that point, but I refused to give up my thirty-five dollars because of seasickness. So I closed my eyes for the remainder of the class. What seemed like two hours was really twenty or twenty-five minutes while I sweated my guts out. At the end of class, I kicked my cleats out of the pedals and pushed people out of my way as I clumsily ran to the bathroom a hundred yards away to promptly throw up in the toilet.

The contents of breakfast no longer in my stomach, I should have felt better, but I only felt worse. So I lay down in my claustrophobic, windowless, ten-by-ten bedroom—where I remained for the rest of the day in the dark.

A knock at 5:00 p.m. startled me back into reality. My sister was at the door.

"Time to get ready for dinner," she said.

"Do I have to go?" I asked.

"Mom and Dad are expecting you," Sabrina said. Kristi lurked in the background. She was dancing to the beat of her own song, humming the words to *Frozen*.

"Auntie Victoria, time to get up. You missed us swimming today," she happily sang.

"Shhh, Kristi. Auntie Victoria isn't feeling well," Sabrina told her.

"No, no, it's OK," I said as I stumbled to the door in the dark, my hands guiding the way. I turned on the light and let them in.

"Oh!" said Sabrina. Her face showed the concern of a parent trying to figure out if I really was OK.

Kristi looked at me in wonderment, fascinated as only a six-year-old could be. "Auntie Victoria, you are green! You look like the leaves of a flower."

"I'm coming," I said. "Let me get my shoes on." I reached into the closet and pulled on a pair of white Nike tennis shoes. Standing, I struggled to put them on while leaning on the wall because my equilibrium was off.

My niece and my sister could tell that I wasn't up to it.

"Are you sure you want to come?" Sabrina asked.

"I must make an appearance. Mom and the family wouldn't be pleased if I didn't show," I said. "But can you please help me down to the dining room?"

"Yes," she said, peering quizzically at me.

She and Kristi led me down the hallway. We saw an older couple walking zigzag ahead of us; we could tell that they were also having difficulty walking because of the waves.

So here are my questions: Why did I feel I must endure this? Why couldn't I set the boundary and say no to my parents?

While we slowly made our way down two floors, making sure that I didn't trip or throw up in the process, I was glad to get out of the room. And when we finally got to our table of eight—a journey which seemed like forty-five minutes but really was maybe fifteen—my dad was glad to see us.

"You made it!" he greeted us cheerfully. "But...oh, you don't look so good," he said to me.

"Do you want some Dramamine?" Aunt Eddie said to me.

"Yes, please. But I've taken four today. Is that too much?" I asked.

My aunt took the package out of her purse and looked at the directions. The words clearly read, "Not to exceed two per day."

"Nah, you should be fine," said Auntie Eddie. "I don't pay attention to the directions."

So I popped two more—my fifth and sixth for the day.

I sat there, savoring my plate of plain rice, while my family ate their decadent meals of Caesar salad, lobster, caviar, chicken, hamburgers, and Baked Alaska over the course of two hours. I finally started to feel better after eating my bland meal. Maybe I'd just needed to eat.

While we all were supposed to do nightly group outing—this night being a reprise of *Starlight Express*—I refrained, deciding instead to take a long walk around the deck where I could savor the cool, salty air. The walk refreshed my body. And my mind told me that I could last for another five days.

However, after I went to my cabin to get some rest, my body said something else. At around two o'clock in the morning, my subconscious decided to wake me. I sat straight up.

This happens occasionally, when my body is stubborn and doesn't want to listen. It's the strong voice I hear when I need reason. I call it the voice of "God" because it comes out of nowhere and startles me. That's how loud it is. And it happens at random occasions. The last time it happened, I was sitting in church and listening to the pastor give his sermon—it was May of 2017. *Victoria, go to USC film school,* the voice said. I had just moved to Los Angeles not even a week prior, and I hadn't yet unpacked all my boxes. The deep, booming voice startled me in the middle of the sermon. *Where the heck did that voice come from? And did others hear it?* I looked around, and apparently, I was the only one who had heard it. So I fiddled with my phone and looked at summer film programs. Soon after, I was accepted into a writing class. That was the last time the voice had talked to me.

And now it was speaking again, two years later—waking me from my restless sleep.

Victoria, you have got to get off this goddamn boat. It doesn't matter how much it costs. It's fucking stupid for you stay on, the voice said.

It was at this point that I started having a full-on dialogue with myself.

"I can do to this. I can endure it," my brain said.

"Why do you want to?" the voice said. "You are miserable. You'd rather be at a client meeting. Even that is more fun and rewarding."

"But this is a family trip. We don't get many trips like this in our lifetimes."

"Are you really having fun? This trip is not a vacation. It's an experiment for you. And ask yourself, is it successful? Did you break any patterns? Did your social experiment work? If it did, get off now, and save yourself."

"I can't. Or, if I did, I'd need a viable excuse because I hadn't finished my social experiment, and I couldn't disappoint my parents."

"You are always sick. Everyone knows you as sick or troubled or having to work. The seasickness is your body's way of revolting against something it obviously doesn't want to do. You want out. I'm here to tell you to listen to your body, because you clearly don't want to save yourself. Think of it this way: throwing up by yourself in your cabin is more fun than hanging out with your family."

If I wasn't seasick, I'd be hanging out with my family. And this was proof that I didn't want to do that. I was a sailor—in Seattle, I had sailed racing boats over the summer, every summer, for ten years. So why exactly was I seasick on an 800-person boat?

At this point, I could see that my subconscious had a point, but I still didn't want to disappoint my parents and my family. I really needed a viable excuse to get out of this cruise and its remaining four days of memories.

As I restlessly slept, tossing and turning, I thought about my experience on the cruise so far. Had my social experiment worked? Had I really broken any patterns while on the boat? I'd seen my mother's tiger-mom traits take on a life of their own—especially at the nightly dinner table. We each had our own form of politeness at the table, an expectation to be on our best behavior and enjoy the time we had together, savoring the light conversations of the day. But, each day, I saw some of the tiger-mom traits come out, like the unconscious tics that people try to hide—the nitpicking of, "That's too much food, Pat," the shaming with a harsh stare toward those who didn't order properly, the acting as if nothing had happened. We all took turns doing this, like taking chocolates from a dish that was passed at the dinner table.

I had successfully said no a few times to activities where we were supposed to create happy family memories. I'd used work as an excuse to get out of a wine tasting, a drink on the lido deck, and watching Kristi and Ann swim. Work became this peaceful solace I could escape to. And my onshore activities were my own because I had deliberately set my boundaries, and my parents hadn't pushed me to join them on shore. I spent time cycling by myself, savoring the unfettered, unspoiled beauty of the wilderness and the smell of pine and fresh, oxygenated air. Or I spent time with my sister and her family, hiking, rock climbing, visiting the glaciers, or whale watching.

I had also gained new insights into my mother. Occasionally, I saw a whole new side of her that I hadn't thought was possible. In those moments, she was no longer the harsh tiger mom I had grown up with. Unlike the mom from my teens, twenties, and early thirties, this tiger mom was fun and relaxed. It was a softer side of her that I had never seen. She became someone who could share and be open to conversation, not just barking orders or making harsh pronouncements.

Maybe it was because both my mother and I had gotten older and were more apt to listen to each other; maybe it was all the years of therapy, energy healing, and heart healing I had done; maybe it was the boundaries I had started to establish in this social experiment. But I realized my mother wasn't as scary as I once thought her to be. She was, in fact, just a sad mother who had probably been tiger-parented herself and didn't know or want anything better, who craved a relationship with her daughter but didn't really understand how to interact with her. I started to understand my mom's patterns, and I realized that that was just how she had been raised. As we grow up, the key to becoming adults is understanding who others really are, and being OK with who we are.

While on the cruise, I had spent a fair amount of time having coffee with my mother, and it had been a treat to get to know her. In our conversations, she'd recounted her daily activities, her hopes, and her dreams.

As I mentioned before, I would typically wake up at around 5:45 or 6:00 a.m. to get in my morning coffee, meditation, and exercise before I started work or went about my day on shore. And it seemed like most days I would run into my mother at the coffee bar after her daily walk. The first day, I thought it was a fluke, but since I never deviated on when I went to the coffee shop, I started to think she had me pegged and was timing her coffee run to coincide with mine.

A typical conversation started with her saying, "Morning, Vic! Fancy you are here at this time. I just got done with my walk." She always met me at 6:30. One time, I arrived a tad late at 6:40, and she was there waiting for me.

"Hi, Mom. Can I buy you a cup of coffee? A latte?" I would say in greeting.

(As passengers, we had to pay additional for our coffee cards in order to get "real" coffee. The cruise served this liquid goo that they pawned off to their passengers as "coffee," but for $120, we would get unlimited real coffee plus fourteen specialty drinks. How had they sold me on the coffee card? The barista at the coffee bar had shown me a large plastic container filled with the brown goo—the color of caramelized poop—and told me they used it for the large canisters of "coffee" at the ship's buffet. I had been instantly sold on the $120 package to get legit coffee.)

"Oh, Vic, you want to buy me a latte? How nice of you," Mom said.

And so it went. Each morning, I'd get her an extra-hot vanilla latte. While we waited for our coffees, she'd dance and do her morning stretches. And while I wished I could be active with her, I'd typically be half asleep and would just yawn and try to do a quick gratitude prayer before my coffee came (typically a double long-pour espresso). Each day, we'd actually had very nice chitchats about life, about what she'd done the day before, why she liked cruises, and what her plans were for the remainder of the year. She'd also talked about how she wanted Sabrina to raise Kristi and Mattie. While my mom wasn't raising her grandkids, she still had certain hopes and dreams for them. During these times, I felt l like we were in a barbershop, just talking about the mundane aspects of life, and it was nice.

When I woke up at 5:30 the next morning, I mused about my revelations and my new fond memories of my mother. I felt complete. The social experiment was no longer needed; I no longer had to participate, nor did I want to. My heart just wanted to be free.

We were to dock in the port of Victoria, British Columbia, at 8:30 a.m., and I was determined to get off the boat—not just to spend the day on shore, but to actually leave the boat with my belongings and to never come back.

After getting up and trying to go for a walk but feeling too ill to do a long one, I headed to the porter. While I was a tad worried that I wouldn't be allowed to leave, I didn't really care much. I had to get off the boat.

"I need to get off the boat today. I've been sick for the last two days," I said to the porter.

The porter, a Filipino in his early thirties, with a haircut that resembled a mop, looked at me with a blank stare. "How may I help you?" he asked.

I repeated myself. "I need to get off the boat today."

"But why?" he asked, his hair flopping as he spoke. "Aren't you having fun?"

"Uh, no," I said.

He blinked twice. "Ma'am, it's not so simple. We need to notify the port authorities. I'll need to notify the manager of your request to leave."

"You can see that I'm green. I tried to work it off this morning, but I'm still seasick. I can't stay on this boat in open seas," I pleaded.

"I don't know if we can get you on the list to leave," he said, this time his Filipino accent coming out. "But we'll see. We can't promise anything."

"So, you're OK to let me suffer on the cruise for the next three days?" I asked.

The porter smiled again. "Ma'am, there's a ship's medic. Perhaps he can help you? And maybe being on land might help?"

I sighed. "I'm leaving the ship without the port authorities' permission."

"We will see what we can do. And, if we can't get you off the ship, we'll be sure to bring the medic around."

While it wasn't a guarantee that I would get off the boat, my mind told me that I'd succeed. I excitedly skipped back the two flights of stairs to my cabin to pack and change. Whether I got permission or not, I was getting off. I turned on my computer and logged on to Expedia, seeing that there was a 4:00 p.m. flight to Seattle. That would leave me enough time to visit the port with Sabrina and the kids and say my brief goodbyes to my family.

I took a quick, five-minute shower and hastily packed my clothes, having a full-blown conversation with myself as I packed. (Keep in mind, this is not the kind of talk you have in your head, but the kind of talk where you're actually talking to yourself out loud.)

"Victoria, you are getting off the boat today."

What if they won't let you off the boat?
"They will."
What will the relatives think?
"Does it matter? You're the color of pea soup that's stuck to a woman's white shirt."
But they are going to be upset.
"Look at yourself. You are miserable. It's for your own sanity."

The dialogue in my head went on and on until the last shoe and garment was packed.

Then I heard a loud knock at the door.

"Auntie Victoria, time to go." Kristi said in her singsong voice.

"Hey, Victoria. We're heading into port now," called my sister.

When I opened the door, Kristi, with her purple jacket, bright smile, and braids, greeted me and tugged at my hand. She then noticed the packed bag.

"Are you leaving today, Auntie Victoria?" she asked.

"Yes, sweetie. I'm leaving today in the afternoon."

"How did you manage that?" Sabrina asked.

"I talked with the porter, and I'm gone," I said.

"You look better, Auntie Victoria," said Kristi. "You can't stay for another few days?"

"No, sweetie," I said to her. "It's time for Auntie Victoria to go, but we'll spend the day together. Is that OK?"

"Can we ride bikes?" she asked.

"Yes, sweetie. My treat," I said.

Sabrina rolled her eyes. "Not sure how you are going to get out of this one, but OK. Let's go. I'm looking forward to good coffee. Let's find the best coffee place in Victoria."

We headed downstairs to leave the boat and spend the day in Victoria. The disembarking process proved to be relatively easy—with the exception of me getting tagged.

As we tried to leave the gangplank, a security guard pulled me aside.

"Ma'am, you can't leave. You need to come with me."

"Go ahead, and let me know which coffee shop. Text me," I told Sabrina.

The guard took me to the Filipino porter's office. He smiled again, but this time with a genuine smile. "Victoria, we were able to put your name on the list. You can leave today. Please leave by 1:30 p.m."

"That's it?" I asked.

"Yes, that's it. Have a good day," he said.

I left, skipping down the gangplank, ready to take on the day. Whenever I had been around my family, I'd felt as if I were an indentured servant, expected to be part of the hive, to ask permission, to participate in groupthink, to pay homage to the family. But once I'd made the decision to leave (and had been given permission to do so), I was able to breathe more easily. I had set a healthy boundary with my family, and I was sticking to it. And, in response, the nausea that I had been feeling lifted like a fog. The fog—the sadness inside of me, the crazy back and forth—left, and I was inspired again.

I spent the day with Sabrina and her family, laughing as we rode our rented bicycles to Charlie's, the famous coffee shop where we got our breakfast and large mugs of coffee. We watched dragon-boat races and walked through the streets of Victoria. It was the freest and lightest I'd felt while on the cruise.

As I thought of an excuse to give my family for why I was leaving, I felt torn. In their eyes, how could I have an acceptable excuse for leaving? How could I hold my ground on what I wanted to do and wanted to say, without having my parents disown me?

I wished I was like my friend Lola, who is a successful attorney at an immigration firm. She once told me how she had broken her tiger-cub pattern early in life at the age of twenty. Her parents had wanted to marry her off to a man who an Asian fortune teller had told them would bring their daughter "good fortune." They'd also wanted her to become a doctor. She came from a long history of MDs—her mother, her brothers, her father, and her grandfather all were doctors, from heart surgeons to pediatricians. But, when in college, she'd preferred the speech and debate classes over biology. While she hadn't been opposed to going into science, she'd realized that she'd have to break the tiger-cub mold early. So she'd decided to study law. The result? Her family didn't talk to her for two years.

Lola had done something that most tiger cubs want to do but don't, because they don't know how to live without communication from their families. To her, the silence from her family was OK, especially as she was going through college. She had broken out of the codependent role a while back when she'd realized that her dependency on her parents' approval had been holding her back from flourishing and doing what she wanted.

Lola aced her LSATs, got accepted to all the top law schools, and received partial scholarships to Harvard, Hastings, and Yale. She was at the top of her class and on the dean's list. She was also valedictorian of her graduating class, and as such, she was responsible for making a speech at graduation. She notified her family about her speech and asked if they'd like to attend. By that time, her family had forgiven her. They were finally OK with her decision. Perhaps it was because she had been named valedictorian? Perhaps it was because she'd also told them that she'd received a scholarship and was going to Hastings, one of the top law schools in the country? I don't know. The result, however, was that she was able to have a relationship with her parents again—on her terms, while doing a career that she had chosen, and while finding someone whom *she* wanted to fall in love with.

As I prepared to tell my family that I was leaving the cruise early, I thought about Lola. I, like most tiger cubs, was afraid to hear what judgment may await me once I set that boundary and stood up for myself. I imagined the whispering, the noncommunication from my family, and the anticipated feeling of isolation.

In the past, when my family had refused to talk to me because I had been deemed as misbehaving or doing something "wrong," the impact had been significant—like a chill on Lake Michigan in the dead of winter. For example, when I was twenty and in college, I would receive care packages with items that reminded me of the warmth of my parents' home—my favorite foods, blankets, and other random gifts. Then, one day, I was cc'd on an email with the aunties in which my parents let them know how well they were doing and how I had been misbehaving. My relatives—cousins, aunts, my sister—cc'd me in their replies but didn't acknowledge me. The comforting phone calls and pleasant conversations I had received from my relatives stopped—dead silence, like the stillness before an earthquake. When they pretended that I didn't exist, and didn't talk to me or acknowledge me, it was like my oxygen had been shut off. I felt like saying, in a strangled voice, "Wait…I'll do whatever you want me to," because I needed that hit of oxygen, that hit of life. For tiger cubs, these passive-aggressive measures are meant to encourage us to see our parents' way. Now, on the cruise, I was forty-five years old and was still afraid of that bite of isolation, that cold shoulder.

Lola had believed in her dream—her vision for herself—and she'd had the courage to step up to her family and stick to her beliefs. And while I aspired to be like her, my version of standing up for myself was a bit messier where, to avoid being judged and/or isolated, I told half-truths about how I felt about the dinnertime conversations, what I was doing with my life, and the sale of my company. And while Lola had made a conscious choice to step up for her beliefs, mine was a knowing, a vision, that motivated me from inside to not quit. And that vision was to eliminate the feeling of seasickness literally and figuratively.

As I approached the ship after the day trip in Victoria, I spotted my aunt and uncle standing in line to board.

I joined them in line, smiling at them while I greeted them. My aunt smiled back at me.

"Hi, Auntie and Uncle. I'm leaving today and will see you back in the Bay Area," I said.

"Vic! Why are you leaving?" Auntie Eddie asked.

"I've been seasick for a few days and can't take it anymore."

"Poor Vic," she cooed. "You've got your dad's stomach."

"Did you see my mom and dad?" I asked.

"No. They might be having lunch in the main restaurant," she said.

We walked in comfortable silence up the gangplank. My mission was to find my mom and dad before I had to leave. I combed the restaurants and the main eating areas to no avail.

I then went to the main eating area and scooped myself two cups of rice and chicken broth.

"Vic!" I heard my aunt's shrill voice. "There you are. Go have lunch with Tom and Kate; they are over there." Her head nodded to the left.

"OK. I only have a few minutes before I leave," I said.

Aunt Eddie looked down at my tray with concern. "You really are sick," she said.

"I wasn't joking," I said, and went off to see my cousin.

"Vic, we shouldn't do this on a boat next time. Or, if it's on a boat, you meet us in port," said Kate. "Of course you'd be sick. You're always sick." She looked from her burger and fries to my meager lunch. "Next time!"

"Thanks, Kate," I said. "If we do this again, it'll be a land trip."

My brain screamed at me when I said it. *Why are you saying that? You don't mean it.*

Yes, I do.

No, you don't.

Yes, I do. They are family.

I shook my head, trying to keep my thoughts from spiraling.

"Vic, are you OK?" Kate asked. "Feeling sick again, even though we're not moving?" She laughed at her own joke.

"No, I'm good. Just trying to get rid of the nausea," I said.

I ate as much rice as I could, and then I excused myself, giving the obligatory hugs and smiles. I went back to my cabin and packed the remainder of my things. Giving it one last go to find my parents, I went to the restaurant, where I spotted my mom and dad with their five-course meal of salad, petite sirloin steak, green peas, potatoes, and chocolate soufflé. My dad saw me.

"Hey, Vic. Come join us," he said. "Oh, you have your things."

I rolled up with my travel bag and backpack. "Hi, Mom and Dad. I wanted to say goodbye before I left. I know that the next four days we're at sea, and I'm too seasick to manage that."

"Oh, you got my stomach," Dad said. "But I don't have problems on boats like this." He bit into his chocolate soufflé.

"Pat, eat your lunch before you eat that," Mom said. She got up from the table. "Well, Vic, we'll miss you. But thank you for joining us for the trip. Get better." She gave me a big hug.

Surprised by her response, I lovingly hugged her. Perhaps it was the morning coffees that had changed our dynamic, but I'd expected some sort of criticism or dig from my mother. Instead, she seemed genuinely concerned for my well-being—in addition to hers.

"What happens to your coffee card?" she asked.

Of course, I knew that she wanted decent coffee for the duration of the cruise, but I hoped that she wanted the card because she would remember all the fond conversations we'd had at our early-morning coffee meetups.

"Mom, do you want it?" I opened my bag and gave it to her.

"Well, if you insist. We'll miss you," she repeated, and she kissed and hugged me for the second time.

After saying my last goodbyes, I left my parents with their half-eaten meals before walking briskly to exit the ship. As I stepped from the gangplank onto shore, I smelled the sea air and found the lone taxi waiting for me on the dock to take me to the Victoria airport. I looked back at the boat as we drove away, feeling proud that I'd had the nerve to stand up for myself and glad that I had gotten off the boat.

While sitting in the Victoria airport and waiting for my flight, I was a tad disappointed in myself because I hadn't completed the cruise. But I was pleased that I had learned all the lessons that I'd need to learn to ensure that the social experiment was a success.

I'd learned that my mother can be funny and unique. I'd also learned that tiger parenting is actually a real experience that many others share—and, more importantly, it can be shaken off at some point when the noose is finally loosened. I'd learned that when people's colorful personalities come out, I tend to shirk from the situation. (Maybe it was a form of PTSD, or maybe it was based on my inability to cope with my family...I didn't know.) And I'd learned that I am capable of changing my behavior and sticking up for myself—and others—when necessary.

The universe rewarded me for my efforts in this experiment of mine. As I sat at the boarding gate, I heard my name on the loudspeaker.

"Paging Ms. Victoria Chan. Can Ms. Victoria Chan come to the A12 desk?" a female voice blared.

As I was deep in thought, the call continued four more times. When I finally realized it was for me, I walked up to the counter.

"Ma'am, can I see your ticket?" asked the smiling, heavyset but jaunty gate agent. She was very perky, and very Canadian, for 2:00 on a Sunday afternoon.

"We're oversold out in Seattle, so I'm getting you a direct flight to San Francisco, if that's OK," she said.

"Yes, that works," I replied.

As the airline attendant gave me my ticket, I looked down at the seat number: seat 2A.

"I think you might have made a mistake," I said and handed her back the ticket. I had bought an economy seat last-minute.

She smiled at me. "That's no mistake at all. I hope you are OK with that. Your San Francisco flight isn't scheduled for another one and a half hours. It won't take off until 5:30 p.m., but you'll get a meal. Enjoy your flight in first class."

"Yes, ma'am. That's totally fine with me!" I exclaimed.

An automatic upgrade. You can't beat that.

Maybe it was just a coincidence, or maybe it was the universe rewarding me for listening to what I truly wanted. I didn't care. I was just glad to be free.

I made my way to the Alaska Airlines lounge, excited and ready to board my flight.

About two days after leaving the cruise, I woke up in my own bed, in the middle of the night, with a realization. It startled me and got me up, urging me to rethink everything that I'd been doing. I've since found that many of us tiger cubs have these revelatory moments. Eventually, you become frustrated that you are living your tiger parents' perception of an "ideal" life, because you know it's just a facade for you. You are fundamentally unhappy with your choices, with living your parents' wants and needs.

One day, you wake up—maybe after a series of sleepless nights—to find that your inner light is burning brightly. You hear a deafening voice directing you to do something, be something, other than what you are right now. Your inner light continues to burn brightly until one day you vomit whatever you really wanted to say—like an excited utterance during a family function about how you really feel about being there. "Hi. I don't want to be here, but I feel obligated, so I'm staying for an hour or two so I don't get ridiculed."

At that point you don't care about anyone's opinions or judgments but your own. You don't care about the shame or the guilt that your family will throw your way when you finally decide to get out of your gilded cage. You are looking for an out from being trapped in the role of the tiger cub, deferring to others, paying respect, and holding your tongue. You are just looking for scenarios where you will be safe and can capture the essence of who you really are.

And that's what had happened to me on the cruise. The deafening noise in my head had become so intense that I'd had to do something to save myself from apologizing for being me, from my mom's harsh words that were considered "love," and from the judgments that my family gave me because I didn't have kids or a spouse. I was tired of feeling less than happy about myself and what I was doing. I knew it wasn't that my parents didn't care about me—they did care, in their own way; that was just how they'd been raised, and they'd learned to raise me and my sister in the same fashion. But I recognized that I had the choice to step away from being a tiger cub, and to be unapologetic for being messily inspirational, balls-to-the-wall, and single while having amazing experiences. Otherwise, my only other choice would be to succumb to the madness and the patterns that came from my family.

Because I had this new perspective, I began rethinking everything that I had been doing, asking myself these questions: *What if I looked around me every day and enjoyed what I did? What if I wasn't so fixated on what the end result would be? What if I didn't have to be desensitized to everything around me? How much richer would my experiences be then? How much happier would I be? Could I just listen to myself to guide my life, as opposed to listening to my family, so that I could have a fuller life?*

While I'd like to say that I zoomed to my potential in those first few days after the cruise, instead I was like a newborn fawn who was unsteady on her legs. And while my social experiment didn't work perfectly, to be quite honest, the results have been mixed. I've had moments where I've felt like I could be myself, use my voice, and voice my opinions. I've taken action on what I wanted to do. But I have also succumbed to that tiger-cub role and have deferred to others. It's only by doing the exercises in this book on a regular basis that I can continue my strategy of breaking away from the tiger-parented cub role.

In addition to the extra four days off from my family because I'd left the cruise early, I took another year off from them, so that I could fully capture the new space I'd created for myself, and so that I could be present and find happiness again without living under the shadow of what my parents wanted for me.

I felt the tugs of loneliness during the free time that opened up after regaining the long hours I used to spend talking to my sister or my mother, and it took time to know exactly what to do with that freedom, to decide what freedom looked like beyond the dynamic that I once knew. I also noticed that I had much more energy than before, and I was able to envision a wider future beyond my tiger mom's vision. During that year off, released from daily reminders of how it was to be a tiger cub, it felt like a weight had left my body. I had the best year in business that I'd ever had; I found love again in a committed relationship; and more economic opportunities came to me. And it was all because I no longer feel the strings of guilt holding me to the family.

Tips for the Tiger Cub

Start journaling about times when you feel like you can show your authentic self (or who you want to be). How often does this happen? Is it daily? Weekly? Monthly? Or do you feel like you're always performing, always showing up as someone else?

Also journal about times when you perform in your life. How often does this happen? What might have happened if you had shown your authentic self in those moments? What would be the worst-case scenario?

Every day, try showing your authentic self for an hour or two and see what happens.

Some self-help experts might suggest writing a mantra one hundred times, like "I am worthy" or "I am perfect in my own skin." But that type of exercise doesn't really align with an Asian upbringing.

Instead, ask yourself: Where has there been push and pull in my life? What has the push and pull been about? Is it about family dynamics? Is it about what I want and what others want?

If the push and pull is about what you want and what others want, where have you suppressed your voice? What does that voice want to say to you? In your evening journal, before you go to bed, write down what that voice wants to say to you. Then write down what it says in the morning. Do this for twenty-one days, and it will give you clues to how you should show up to live your authentic life and experience freedom from the binds of your tiger mom.

CHAPTER 7

Lessons Learned by a Tiger Cub

WHILE THE EXPERIENCE OF being tiger-parented is riddled with years of self-criticism, self-doubt, anxiety, and distrust, I've also come to appreciate the valuable lessons that come from being raised by a tiger mom. In this chapter, I've listed what I've learned from my tiger mom and from talking with many other tiger cubs. I encourage you to think back on your experiences and reflect on what positive lessons you've inherited from your own tiger mom.

1. *We've learned to treat money with respect.*

If we've learned but one thing, it is to respect and hold on to our money. Being poor—not being self-sufficient—is among the highest forms of shame in the tiger mom's view, especially if she has to tell her friends about it. Money is a marker of your success, and it's an important piece in ensuring your peace and security now and into the future. As such, it should always be treated with respect as the valuable resource it is.

For as long as I can remember, my mother taught me and my sister about the importance of savings. We learned about long-term savings (i.e., money that you can't touch until you are over sixty-five), medium-term savings (money that can be accessed if you need it but that should rarely be touched, such as stocks, bonds, house equity, and rental property), and short-term savings (money that you set aside for a rainy day that can be touched for vacations, etc.). This approach has benefited me immensely as it has taught me about financial freedom and the importance of being able to access money when I want and/or need it.

2. *We are not afraid of frugality.*

We've also learned to be frugal so that we can have money later. This includes saving and reusing plastic bags, using spaghetti jars as storage containers, reusing plastic containers from restaurants, saving coins to roll into one-dollar and five-dollar increments, and wearing designer hand-me-downs. When I was ten, I walked to the bank with a large backpack, proud to covert my change—over fifty dollars—into bills. With the money, I was able to buy a gift for my father's birthday.

3. *We understand the value of planning ahead so we can achieve financial security.*

I learned from my mother that creating a financial plan, following the plan, saving, and investing against the plan (which includes the diversification of money and asset classes) could help not only later in life but also in cases of emergencies.

In being taught to plan ahead to safeguard our financial futures, we were told to always have a Plan A, Plan B, and Plan C. For example, when I got married, I had several plans in place to ensure that I would be protected in case of a disaster (such as divorce). Like many tiger parents, my parents had saved their money to ensure that both Sabrina and I would have down payments for our houses. As part of that, my parents cosigned for my mortgage, and their names were on the deed to my house. I, of course, thought that this was a terrible idea. I wanted my parents' names off the deed and the mortgage because I thought my husband's (at the time) name should be on both documents. But my parents held steadfast. Fast-forward eight years, and their plan paid off when I got divorced. Having their names on the deed was the only way that I didn't have to pay my ex half of all our assets. (I would have paid him even less money had I not taken equity out of the house to buy another house.) While I learned other money-saving and money-making strategies later in my late thirties and early forties, I'm pleased to say that, because of my planning and forethought, I am finally set later in life in the event of injury—even with errant spending on trivial things like wine, travel, and living large.

4. *Everything we do is driven by the imperative to succeed.*

Graduate-level work and career success are also positive by-products of being raised by a tiger parent. While we had the strictest of childhoods growing up, many of us tiger cubs never questioned whether we would go to college and have high-paying jobs. It was expected that we'd graduate in three years if fortunate, four years if we needed to, and then go back to school to get an MBA, an MA, or a doctorate. We'd then go on to establish ourselves by excelling in our chosen professions.

I excelled in public relations, owning my own successful agency within seven years of starting in the profession. I even excelled as a lawyer, even though my parents disapproved of me getting my law degree and practicing law. During my time as a practicing attorney, I had won the largest case against the State of Washington for sexual assault. I had also successfully negotiated a case on behalf of my parents with their insurance company. My parents' home is on a street that curves, and one day, at around 4:00 a.m., the driver of an Acura MDX had fallen asleep at the wheel (probably after having too much to drink) and had a freak accident. The car jumped the curb in front of my parents' house, smashed their gate, and went into the front of the house through the window in my old bedroom. It ultimately landed on my old bed. The driver, of course, tried to run, but it was futile given the loud noise and hypervigilant neighbors who called 911. Dealing with the paperwork between the insurance companies became overwhelming, and my mother, fearful of getting ripped off by the insurance lawyers and her own insurance company, called me in to do the negotiation—a crook dealing with crooks. After that, I received no more heckling from my mom about receiving a law degree; she finally saw the usefulness of that "awful" degree.

While I no longer practice law, I have since incorporated my experience practicing litigation into my public relations practice when I'm representing some of the foremost legal technology brands.

New Paths for Tiger Cubs

1. Be grateful for what you have.

These last few lessons I've learned by finding contrasts to my tiger-parented upbringing. Being grateful for everything we have is not a given in the Asian culture. So, to counteract that, I take time every day to write about everything I have to be grateful for. I put together a list of everything that I've done and it helps me to realize that I've done a lot in my short life. And I don't necessarily need to be where I (or my family) think I am supposed to be. For example, I'm grateful that I have the drive to succeed—even now, at the age of forty-nine. I'm grateful that I have the ambition to be seen and the courage to do the things that I do. I'm grateful that I have the courage to be seen as who I truly am. I'm grateful that I am capable of multitasking, and that I can understand how to put things together. I'm grateful for my parents, my family, and the people who have helped me become the person that I am today. Unlike the patterns that I experienced growing up that taught me to continuously feel dissatisfied, these lessons of gratitude have taught me to be content. In all these times, my tiger parenting helps me and does not limit me from my potential.

2. Free the mind from judgment.

Judgment is an Asian thing. We judge everything, from the table in front of us, to our friends, to who we are as people.

When have you not seen the tiger mom's glare, the evil eye, or the blank stare because she disapproved? However, when we can break free from that judgment, we can see that whatever is in front of us is not necessarily good or bad; it just is. This is an important lesson to learn because, if you hold on to judgment, it will haunt you and will prevent you from moving forward, from doing anything at all. If you can free your mind from judgment and realize that life just is—that the table in front of you is not "bad" or "good" or "too cheap"—then you can see things for what they are.

To be in judgment limits you from experiencing all of life by limiting your ability to see the beauty and opportunities that may be right in front of you. One of my former mentors, Drew Neagle, always talks about a story that took place when he was helping in a warehouse. For two years, he wanted to make more money; however, he didn't see an opportunity to do so. He made the decision to change his mindset and act as if he loved what he was doing. Over the two-year period, one of the oil haulers whom he talked with at the warehouse kept telling him that he could double his money by working to haul oil. The problem was that Drew was so set in judgment that he didn't see the opportunity as his. The day that Drew changed his mindset was the day that he actually heard for the first time that the opportunity was available for him. Within forty-eight hours of pursing the opportunity without judgment hindering him, he doubled his income. Being judgment-free opens you up to experiencing the present, without the limitations you put on yourself.

3. *Be seen as you.*

Each time you make friends with a person or start dating a person, they have to get to know you. That means sorting through your layers of "muck"—the hurt from your childhood, the obsessive need to be liked, the "wants" instilled in you from your parents, the personality that's been left unformed due to your family's expectations—to see and understand who you really are as a person. This is true to some extent for everyone, but with tiger cubs, it becomes especially difficult to break that shell because that armor of "muck" is on so tight that it's hard to pry off. You become so entangled with your family's dynamics and what they think of you—along with the ever-present parental disapproval—that you learn to suppress your true creativity. Being seen for who you truly are—your authentic, vulnerable self with a life that your parents can't imagine because they haven't lived it—is just foreign. And when you go against the grain of who your parents want you to be, well, that's when all hell breaks loose.

For me, this has been a balancing act of capturing my free time and remaining free from judgment and harsh words from my mother, my aunts, my sister, and my cousins while still finding my place in my family. And, to be quite honest, while I'm getting better at it, I still sometimes struggle. There's still a lot to learn, and I'm still learning how to show up as my true self.

How do you know when it's time to stand up for yourself in your Asian family? When you realize that everything around you has been dreamed for you or done for you. When there's a feeling that you owe them—out of respect because they are your elders, because they saw you grow up and groomed you, and because their opinions matter more than your own. When you don't feel heard. When you feel like you are a puppet with your parents being the puppeteers. This is when it's time to make significant changes to start being seen as you—the authentic you that can have a voice of your own. Being authentically you (without the tape of your parents' voices running through your head) can make a wealth of difference for your happiness and contentedness, the choices you make, or the relationships you keep with your loved ones. And you can do it at any age. You, too, can do what I did and know that it's time to stand up for yourself now.

Tips for the Tiger Cub

It's time to admit to yourself that being tiger-parented hasn't been all bad.

In what areas of your life has being tiger-parented benefited you?

In what areas of your life has being tiger-parented hindered you? In the areas where it hindered you, what corrective courses of action can you take now?

Write a description of yourself—not of your accomplishments, but of your traits and characteristics of who you are as person. Do you like what this description says? If you don't, how would you change it?

Lastly, write your obituary. Who are you as a person? What are your accomplishments? What is your legacy? What do you need to do to reconcile who you are now with what you want to be known as? Create a vision map for your legacy.

Epilogue

AFTER THE CRUISE, WHILE I was taking another year away from my family, I spent time reflecting on everything that had changed since I began this journey of releasing my tiger-parented bonds. In learning about my mom's past and getting to know her on a deeper level, I had gained new insights into her role—and mine—in the dynamic between the tiger mom and her tiger cub. I'd also developed a keen awareness of how control, criticism, and perfectionism had shaped who I was. And I was now thriving as the new, authentic version of myself, free from those constraints. I also had several tools at my disposal—the meditations, journaling practices, and self-reflection exercises in this book—to help me identify the negative epigenetic patterns within my family and set boundaries that prioritized my well-being.

From this new perspective, I was ready to reintegrate with my family because I could now recognize those old, familiar patterns from a mile away. And I wanted to start by meeting with my twin sister. I had missed her. I mean, how could I not? We had been stuck at the hip since birth. During that year apart, my heart had ached for her because, in fact, she was a part of me. I had grown up with her in the womb, and we were "womb-mates." So I decided to contact her.

On the fateful day that I reconnected with Sabrina, I made the journey into San Francisco to meet her in the Noe Valley. Sabrina had managed to find a very chic little restaurant that had organic ingredients, was well-rated, and was gluten-free. I arrived first and sat at a window table, where I immediately spotted Sabrina walking in.

"Sabrina!" I went over to her and hugged her, a welcome embrace after almost a year of not talking.

Ever demure and polite, Sabrina said, "You know, we didn't have to meet as I know that your year with Drew Neagle is not over. I don't want to be the deterrent to any positive changes you're making."

I knew that she was concerned—overly concerned—that she would detract from the learnings of my mindset coach, Drew Neagle. For the past year, he had been working with me to overcome some of the family and business challenges that had been preventing me from experiencing abundance. It had been the most glorious year where I was free from judgment, from disapproving comments, and from unconsciously competing with my sister, my aunts, and my family. I was learning to be 100 percent authentic and utterly me. I wasn't making excuses for my choices. I wasn't apologizing for being me. It was utter bliss.

Epilogue

"Nonsense," I said. "I wanted to see you. And besides, I can handle you, just not Mom."

As we proceeded to talk during dinner, I could see the struggle that my sister was going through, the chaos in her field that she'd brought with her. I picked up on the conflicting emotions of judgment, openness, and curiosity that she felt about my success up to that point.

That dinner with my sister turned out to be a good reference point for me because, even though I enjoyed seeing her and being with her (she's my twin and my best friend, for heaven's sake), I knew I still needed some more time before I was ready to face the rest of my family again.

So I proceeded to not talk with my sister or my parents for another six months, which allowed me the time I needed to heal further. This time, the healing process wasn't anything like all the previous work I had done with healers. I didn't lay on a table to receive energy work; I didn't clear myself with crystals. I just literally sat with myself and got to know myself better. I made an effort to fall in love with myself. I learned that I wasn't a bad person for giving myself the things that I wanted. I wasn't selfish. I wasn't being disrespectful to my family. I experienced joy—pure joy—without the fear or judgment or criticism that I would normally get from my family.

And, eventually, I felt ready to see my family again. It was at this point that I deployed my emotional guards, the protectors of my soul. OK, that's an exaggeration, but I did need exercises to help me with my family. I did energy movement once or twice a week to stay connected to myself. And I became one of those new age freaks, meditating for the sake of meditating, and so that I could stay grounded while being with my family. And, to be fair, that is what kept me sane—and is still keeping me sane.

Now, I touch base with my family on (what I would call) a regular basis. To some, it may appear that it's not the best of relationships—one where I talk with my sister two or three times a week and my parents as necessary—but it allows me to be connected and disconnected at the same time, so that I can stay in the energy flow that I'd learned and stay focused on the goals that I had set out a while ago.

Several months after I'd started talking with my family again, I found out that my mother had finally asked my sister why I had taken that year off.

Sabrina, being ever so stalwart, had mustered the courage to tell her about her experience with our mother. Sabrina explained that she felt our mother questioned her all the time about her morals, her values, and the way she was raising her kids. She said she felt demoralized from her conversations with Mom, and that she continually had to argue with her and defend her actions. My sister was finally starting to find her voice after all these years.

"Mom, I can't really talk for Victoria, but I feel like I always have to prioritize your feelings over the feelings of my own children and the needs of my own family. And it makes

Epilogue

me question how I raise my family because you don't approve. And you show your disapproval."

"We are still your parents, Sabrina," said Mom. "We still have the right to parent you. We still have the right to question you and give you direction."

At that point, Sabrina had an aha moment, and it made sense to her why—to that day—our parents were still voicing their large opinions. And, with that realization, Sabrina started to speak her truth and set a new boundary. "Mom, you do not have that right. That right ended when we were eighteen. I allow you to speak your opinion; I care about what you have to say, and I appreciate that you care about our welfare, but this is not a right you have. It's a privilege that I give you, not the other way around."

At that point, Mom was speechless. After years of conforming to our tiger mom's wishes, my sister had finally stuck up for herself.

When Sabrina told me about her conversation with our mother, I began to see that, by making subtle shifts toward healthier relationships, we were creating ripple effects within the greater family dynamic. While it was clear that our mother had closed herself off to change and would never have the capacity for the emotional bond we wanted, Sabrina and I were learning to recast our roles in our interactions with Mom. And, in doing so, we were modeling new family patterns for the next generation.

To step outside of those old patterns is huge—for yourself, and for the rest of your family. To say, "I choose to be happy; I choose to not succumb to the doubters; I choose to be confident in my own choices" does not come naturally to us tiger cubs. And yet that abundance is out there; it's just waiting for you to start making changes. You have to see it, and be confident in your innate ability, and then step into who you are truly meant to be.

You can find this freedom in your own life. I hope that the tips I've shared here will help you break out of the intergenerational tiger-cub cycle of striving, working hard, and being punished. It is *your time* to find emotional stability, accomplish your goals, and discover your vision of who you want to be. And the best part is that you can do all of this while maintaining your bonds with your family. I wish you a bright new future!

About the Author

VICTORIA HA IS KNOWN for her insightful writings on success, self-discovery, and the effects of tiger parenting. Her journey, from a prodigious youth in music and academics to a successful attorney and marketer, inspires others to break free from entrenched patterns and embrace their true selves amid cultural expectations. Her work has appeared in *Forbes, Fast Company, Entrepreneur,* and *Medium.*